ROB SHIRLEY

FOUNDER OF

MASTERCRAFT BOATS

BY

JON BRODERICK

PUBLISHED BY LEMON PRESS
ACWORTH, GA
WWW.LEMONPRESSPUBLISHING.COM

1ST EDITION

Lemon Press Publishing
PO BOX 459
Emerson, GA 30137

DEDICATION

The MasterCraft Story could never have been told but for the generosity of Terry McNew and the MasterCraft Boat Company.

Rob Shirley led a team of dedicated family and friends in the creation of the MasterCraft Brand. Many of their stories and accomplishments are chronicled within these pages, and many of those dedicated and loyal members of the MasterCraft family are no longer with us. But, their efforts live on in the perfection they have helped to create, and in the memories of those who knew them, worked with them and shared in the accomplishments of the entire MasterCraft experience.

Jon Broderick
Author

ANDY MAPPLE

NOVEMBER 3, 1962-AUGUST 22, 2015

FORWARD

PAUL CHAPIN PRESIDENT
USA WATER SKI EDUCATIONAL FOUNDATION

Words like water skier, boat builder, designer, innovator, promoter, family man, and friend, are among many that describe Rob Shirley. When Rob first introduced his 18-foot MasterCraft inboard to the world on July 4th, 1968, he changed the towboat scene with "a revolutionary new tournament ski boat designed and built by a tournament skier for the ultimate in tournament performance".

With his extensive knowledge of boats he was not afraid to push the limits and design a boat that embodied everything a skier could ask for, and at a price that a middle-income skier could afford. His engineering and performance designs over the years produced a boat that had a perfect table for trick skiing, a low profile high speed wake with minimal spray for slalom skiing and dual and triple fins for better tracking that helped enable records to be set. He was not afraid to set the trend towards styling with stars and stripes and metal flake that made each boat standout.

His forward thinking, out of the box philosophy led to the first all stainless tow bar, new hull designs, new and different interiors. Rob Shirley's longer and wider boats also combined with larger props and gear ratio changes that led to more power and efficiency and ultimately, a tremendous towboat. He also produced an outboard version of the MasterCraft for the accomplished recreational skiing market.

Rob was a major player behind the pro water ski tour that gave the sport weekly TV coverage and made many of the top skier's stars in their own right. Rob's influence on boat building and on water skiing forever changed the sport and the new Master Craft Boat Company continues his legacy as they build boats for all towed water sports.

Paul Chapin President
USA Water Ski Educational Foundation

THE FUTURE OF MASTERCRAFT

BY TERRY MCNEW
CEO MASTERCRAFT BOAT COMPANY

Rob Shirley founded MasterCraft in 1968 with a vision of creating the best ski boat in the industry. He accomplished that and established a foundation that would create the best-known brand in the Performance Sport Boat category within the overall boating industry.

Today we continue to build on that legacy. MasterCraft currently has 12 models in its portfolio, the most of any brand in the Performance Sport Boat category. Anchoring our line-up is the Prostar three-event ski boat along with 11 other models that support wakeboarding, wake surfing and general recreational boating.

MasterCraft is an iconic brand synonymous with quality, innovation and performance, built around the brand pillars of Legacy, Power, Precision and Progression.

Legacy refers to our rich heritage defined by an engaged and innovative culture since 1968. Power stands for the fact MasterCraft is recognized for superior performance, with a number of world records set and championships won using MasterCraft boats. Precision translates into significant resale premiums and backed by the most comprehensive warranty in the industry. Progression signifies MasterCraft as an industry leader in innovation and achievement with numerous recent technological innovations and industry awards.

Today MasterCraft is as strong as it's ever been. We recently took the company public and we're listed on the NASDAQ exchange under the ticker symbol MCFT. We're now completely debt free which sets us on course for a very bright future. With 135 dealers worldwide selling our boats in 40 countries, MasterCraft truly is a global brand.

The MasterCraft difference is made up of four components. It combines 1) an aspirational, iconic brand synonymous with quality, innovation and performance with 2) an industry-leading Product Development & Engineering process 3) highly efficient product development and manufacturing systems and 4) brought to market with differentiated sales and marketing capabilities. Today we release three brand new models every year supporting a portfolio of 12 unique models. No one in our segment has that combination. It's a disruptive model and one that I believe our competitors will have a difficult time matching.

Rob started a unique company in 1968 and 47 years later we're continuing that legacy and positioning it for the next generation to continue its success for years to come. Master-Craft is dedicated to designing, engineering and building the best boat on the water for families to enjoy exceptional experiences together. We may build boats, but at the end of the day we're in the business of bringing enjoyment and a lifetime of memories to people around the world.

TERRY MCNEW AND ROB SHIRLEY AT THE MASTERCRAFT FACTORY 2015

CHAPTER ONE

1953-1959

The golden age of water skiing began in 1953 when Esther Williams water-skied across the silver screen in the movie houses across the country. The movie, 'Easy to Love', was filmed at Cypress Gardens and starred Van Johnson and Esther Williams and the background and theme of the movie became the water ski capitol of the world.

MOVIE POSTER FROM EASY TO LOVE FILMED AT CYPRESS GARDENS 1953 STARTING THE GOLDEN AGE OF WATER SKIING

Shortly after 'Easy To Love' hit the big screen, boat sales and water skiing became increasingly popular on the lakes and rivers all over the United States, and water skiers soon were testing their skills in competition, forming ski clubs and performing water ski shows to attract even more attention to the sport.

Live television stars brought their shows to Cypress Gardens to broadcast sunshine, flowers and water skiers in the background. But the skiers and the powerful towboats were often able to put the TV stars in the background. The Today Show with Dave Garroway, Peter Lynd Hayes, Arthur Godfrey, Carol Burnett and many others came to the Gardens and ended up playing second fiddle to the talented pioneer skiers of that era.

1960-1968 THE EARLY YEARS

ENTREPRENEUR ROB SHIRLEY

By 1960, a young man named Rob Shirley had already become an expert water skier and worked for Custom Craft Boats of Virginia. Rob earned a reputation for driving their runabout boats in marathon races of 100 miles or more. Rob, more often than not, won most of those races. He also learned how to construct fiberglass boats and became an expert of the molding process used in the forming and shaping of boat hulls. Rob Shirley was mechanically inclined and would soon be using those skills to change the ski boat world, as it was known at that time.

Home for Rob was in the Smokey Mountains of East Tennessee. Rob attended high school in Alcoa, Tennessee. His early athletic achievements were in football but his passion was for water skiing. Rob's father bought a 16-foot Crosby outboard that he rigged with twin 45 horse-power Mercury Motors. It was an ideal ski boat in its day. Rob did not own a car, but many of his friends did, with trailer hitches. Water skiing bonds were formed early and last forever. Rob had the ideal job with Blount Outboard Marine in Maryville as a rigger. Boats would come from the factory with no windshield, motor or steering wheel. He would soon become good friends with Norm Goodson who was the chief mechanic at Blount Marine, and who taught Rob how to properly install steering systems, outboard motors and windshields on all of the boats that came in. Rob and Norm learned to barefoot ski the hard way by falling at 50 miles per hour and figuring out that 35 miles per hour hurt a lot less. Rob and Norm might have seen a water ski show and heard the announcer proclaim barefoot speeds in excess of 50 miles per hour, as they often did. One should never believe the stories and exaggerations made by show ski announcers about boat speeds and jumping distances.

NORM GOODSON AND ROB IN THEIR 1955 BUICK BEACH BUGGY

PATROLLING FLORIDA BEACHES IN 1963

Rob reminisced with World Champion Ken White years later about almost being expelled from high school for skipping school to go water skiing. The only reason they didn't expel Rob was that he was a key player on the Alcoa Varsity football team. That is when he found out that he and Ken had been classmates at Alcoa when they were both 10 years old. Ken was a star show skier and a world champion tournament skier years later.

In 1959, Rob enrolled in college at East Tennessee State University in the school of Architecture. He soon decided that a desk job was not for him and that the pay didn't suit his anticipated lifestyle. He got married, left school and headed for West Palm Beach with his new bride, Flo, where they became members of the Ski Club of the Palm Beaches. It was a thriving club with many world class champions, such as Jimmy "Flea" Jackson and Noreen Bardill, Roland "Red" Davies, along with his son Rollie, and many others.

Rob soon found a job with a road surveying crew and spent many days wandering in the swamps west of the Palm Beaches surveying land for the construction of Intestate 95. A few months later, he landed a job with Pratt & Whitney Aircraft as a draftsman and Flo was hired as a stenographer. The Shirley's enjoyed a comfortable combined family income and spent all of their free time on the water competing in every local or regional water ski tournament and performing in countless club water ski shows.

But Rob wanted more. He took some time off from Pratt & Whitney to start his own water ski school, knowing he was welcome back at Pratt & Whitney anytime if it didn't work out. He was determined that his goal would be achieved. He didn't realize the convoluted direction it would take in the process.

CHAPTER TWO

TAKING CHANCES

In the early 60's, Rob and Flo Shirley were eager and enthused to try anything to make the water skiing business a success. Robby met a man in Palm Beach that mentioned he was a partner in a new hotel that was being built in Freeport on Grand Bahama Island. He invited Rob to open a Bahamian ski school during the slow months in West Palm Beach.

Rob informed Norm Goodson about the Bahamas offer and they decided to give the Freeport adventure a try. Norm and Rob took Rob's 16-foot Crosby with the twin Mercury outboard engines out into the open sea and headed east for the 60 miles to Freeport from West Palm Beach, using nothing but a rusty compass. It was a crazy venture that had every opportunity to fail, but didn't; at least not right away.

The venture lasted only a couple of months. Norm and Rob had very little overhead and were charging $60.00 per hour, living high on the hog in the Bahamian Paradise. It was a good thing that Flo kept her job at Pratt & Whitney, because Norm and Rob were about to leave their room at the plush hotel on Lucaya Beach when the adventure ended abruptly with a phone call. A man with a gravelly voice and a threatening accent informed Rob that he had better leave the Bahamas in the next 24 hours or the life of Rob's wife would be in immediate peril, along with their own. The man on the phone even named her and knew where she worked.

Real or not, Rob and Norm took the threat seriously and left Freeport right away, shipping the boat and everything they owned on the next airplane headed for Florida.

Months later, Rob saw an article in Life Magazine about some skiers that were running a ski school on Lucaya Beach Grand Bahama. They had discovered a sunken ship near Freeport that was loaded with millions in gold coins. The rumor that followed that story reported that those men were all killed while trying to smuggle those gold coins into the United States from the Bahamas. It is unclear as to whether or not the threatening voice on the phone was the actual killer, or if whoever was the killer thought that Rob and Norm were his actual target. It is a Grand Bahamian drama that Rob and Norm safely avoided by leaving the island.

After the Freeport incident, Norm Goodson accepted a job at Tuppen's Marine in Lake Worth and Rob was asked by Leo Benz to run his water ski school in Miami. Leo Benz was a practicing attorney in Miami and owned Lee's Ski School. A few months later Hurricane Cleo hit Miami and Rob hurried to secure all the boats and equipment at the ski school and then drive through the storm to West Palm Beach where his wife was giving birth to their first child, Jill in 1964.

ROB SHIRLEY BAREFOOTING IN HIS EARLY DAYS IN TENNESSEE

By the time 1965 rolled around, Rob had leased a parcel of land from the Lake Worth Parks & Recreation Department on Lake Osborne for his water ski school operation. Rob trained hard to become a respectable water ski jumper and a rated master slalom skier. His best jump was 135 feet and he was making consistent runs through the slalom course on a short-line 45 feet long under the old rules of competition. He had spent every weekend participating in tournaments. Rob was a paid performer in the Tommy Bartlett Water Ski Shows that summer of 1965 at the Wisconsin Dells in Wisconsin. Rob was hired by Bartlett show director Jack Wylie and performed with Skip Gilkerson, both future Water Ski Hall of Fame honorees. Rob and Flo lived in a tent on the grounds of the Wisconsin Dells attraction.

Leo Bentz of Miami was the "inventor" of the Ski Nautique. He made and used the first few models of this water ski inboard before selling the rights to manufacture to Correct Craft. Leo was inducted into the Florida Water Ski Federation Hall of Fame 2003 after already achieving the Award of Distinction in 1995.

At that time however, Leo was operating a highly successful ski school in Miami Beach and he continued his interest in water skiing while attending law school and later as a practicing attorney. He has retired from competitive water skiing.

After hurricane Cleo, Rob considered leaving the ski school business and returning to his old job at Pratt & Whitney. But the water ski business was in his blood and Rob decided to give the business of a water ski school another try. He negotiated for a parcel of land on Lake Osborne in West Palm Beach and started Robby's Ski School.

ROB SHIRLEY'S FIRST SKI SCHOOL BOAT AT LAKE WORTH, FLORIDA

Robby's Water Ski School in Lake Worth, Florida was well known for the enthusiasm of its owner, Rob Shirley, and his growing reputation in local water ski competitions. Rob, and several members of his group, became welcome visitors in the international tournaments that were being held at Cypress Gardens and at other ski clubs in the Southern Region of the American Water Ski Association (Now USA Water Ski).

ROBBY'S SKI SCHOOL ADVERTISEMENT

Rob was one of the first to be invited to trailer his boat to other tournaments. He had an early edition of the Ski Nautique boats built by Correct Craft Boat Company in Orlando, Florida. Rob may have very well been the first boat owner to use his personal boat as a promotional model on behalf of a ski boat manufacturer. The boat had a smaller wake, used less fuel and was fast becoming a favorite of all of the tournament water skiers, including national and world champions of the sport.

Rob promoted his idea for creating credit courses at local colleges in Physical Education and worked to obtain contracts with Palm Beach Junior College and expanded to include Miami Dade South Campus and Indian River College. The credit courses became so popular that there was a waiting list to take Rob Shirley's classes. Each college provided a professor of Physical Education and Rob would lecture on water sports and boating safety one or two times each week. Each student paid premium tuition for the courses and Rob received his money in advance for each course.

Back at his ski school, Rob trained skiers, and built up his team of accomplished tournament skiers. He earned an exceptional income for his off-season college classes and an even better income during the tourist season from the wealthy Palm Beach water ski enthusiasts that visited his school in the winter months.

By late 1965, Rob bought several new Correct Craft Nautique boats and hired employees to drive them at the ski school. He was still providing most of the ski instruction. Rob was having trouble with one of his Correct Craft boats. When the ski bar that was attached to the floor of Rob's boat tore out, the manufacturer refused to help with any repairs. It was during this period that Rob decided to build his own boat using improved standards of construction.

CHAPTER THREE

ARDEN "ART" COZIER

In the summer of 1966, Art Cozier had a day job at RCA in the West Palm Beach area. Art and his friends water-skied every weekend. The boat that Art owned in those early years was a 15-foot Fibercraft with a Mercury 50 horsepower motor that failed to pull up some of his heavier friends. Doing step-starts with a slalom ski off the beach caused the skiers to sink to their waists before the boat gained enough speed to get the ski to plane off on top of the water. Art and his friends had been skiing on the Intracoastal Waterway. The Intercoastal, as the locals called the waterway, wasn't a great place to ski because luxury yachts would throw huge wakes that wreaked havoc with water conditions. Art and his skiing mates didn't know the area very well which led to some pretty spectacular groundings of the boat on various sand-bars. Soon they discovered Lake Osborne in Lake Worth, which was far more comfortable. It was surrounded by a County park, which meant there were picnic tables, restrooms, and decent boat ramps. For Art and his friends, the lake was a great place to ski.

Art tells the story about one day in particular when, "Over in one corner of the lake, we noticed that there was a group of skiers doing all sorts of neat things, like going over a ski jump, flying kites, and pulling multiple skiers together behind the same boat."

Art also noticed that some of these people skied with a particular type of boat that didn't have an outboard motor, but instead, had an inboard-mounted engine. Obviously there was plenty of power to do whatever they wanted. Art decided right then that he wanted that type of a boat. Art soon learned that it was a Correct Craft, and set out to find one for sale, but could not locate anyone who knew where there might be one. One of his friends had met a member of the South Dade Ski Club in Miami who worked at a marine supply in Miami called KGS Marine. Art's friend called KGS Marine and asked the counterman, Jerry, whether he knew where one could see a Correct Craft for sale. Jerry said that he didn't know of any such boat in the area, but that there happened to be a customer in front of him who might be able to help us. He handed the phone across the counter and Art recalls his first conversation with Leo Bentz. Leo Bentz, who not only ran a ski school in North Miami Beach, but also had built the first Ski Nautique. Furthermore, Leo had a used Ski Nautique for sale. Art bought Leo's boat and headed to Lake Osborne with his ski buddies.

The boat Art Cozier bought from Leo still had LEE'S SKI SCHOOL painted on both sides in big letters. Soon after launching the boat, we were approached by a man driving a boat that looked identical to the one Art had just bought, except it was a different color.

He called out to Art, "Hey, you guys, I run the ski school on this lake and I intend to be the only ski school on this lake. Why are you guys here?"

Art quickly explained to him that he had just bought the boat, and would soon be taking the lettering off the sides of the boat.

And that is how Art Cozier first met Rob Shirley.

ART COZIER RUNNING TESTS ON MASTERCRAFT BOAT # 1

After Art bought a similar boat to those that the group of skiers on Lake Osborne was using, he started paying more attention to what they were doing, and of course wanted to try some of their advanced skills. Art joined them for some of their activities. Before long he became one of the regulars hanging around the ski school, and even began driving for Rob when he came early on weekends to practice his own skiing. That led to his helping him teach skiing when he was needed, driving for him when he needed to assist novices by skiing with them, and generally helping out around the ski school.

Art Cozier became fairly close to Rob and his family. When the owner of the house that he had been renting told Art that he needed to move back into his house immediately, Rob invited Art to bunk at Rob and Flo's home until he could find another place to live.

The Florida National Guard rudely interrupted Art's summer. Art was a member for the requisite two weeks' Summer Field Training. Finding a new place to live would have to wait. Art packed off for his two weeks with the Guard. When he returned, Art went to Rob's house to drop off his equipment, looked out the back window and saw, laying on the grass in his back yard, the complete deck from Rob's Ski Nautique.

"What could possibly be going on here?" Art thought, as he ran out the door to go looking for Rob. He first went to the ski school, and got another surprise. The engine from the Ski Nautique was hanging on a chain hoist hooked to a tree branch, and Rob was nowhere to be found. Soon a member of the ski group showed up. Art asked, "Where's Rob, and why am I finding major parts of his boat here and there?"

Art was shocked to learn that Rob was in Boynton Beach building a new boat at Brandt Boat Company. Art couldn't get there fast enough! He simply had to see what was going on. Art walked in just as Rob was making some tough decisions.

CHAPTER FOUR

ROB'S FIRST ATTEMPT TO BUILD A BOAT

What Art walked in on that day at The Brandt Boat Company was a genius creating history. Rob was deciding, should he take the time to construct a plywood *plug* (the positive shape of the boat he intended to build to shape the mold), or take the easier route and use his own Ski Nautique for a base-mold and then make changes to the hull? Rob decided that it would be less costly and time consuming to use the Ski Nautique as his base. His plan included cutting his former ski boat in half to make the new hull longer, and split it down the middle to make it wider. In order to build a new boat, Rob sacrificed his old one to do so. Only a dedicated water skier with an entrepreneurial spirit would understand such a sacrifice. Rob's entrepreneurial spirit was committed.

Rob's wife, Flo and other loyal skiers and trusted friends supplied hundreds of hours of labor by sanding the plug and cutting materials for the new boat. Names from the past like Johnny Alvaroe, a colorful and regular friend of the early days in the ski tournament crowd, (may he rest in peace) and Arden Art Cozier, a bastion of respect to this day in water skiing history at Master Craft and now with Correct Craft Boats, as well as Bill Caldwell, another great name from the golden age of skiing. (May he also rest in peace). Rob's marriage to Flo was put to the test as she wore out hundreds of sheets of sandpaper working on the form of Rob's new boat, and endured many late hours afterward when Rob finally returned home utterly exhausted.

The newly modified boat was crafted at night in Gary Brandt's boat shop. Gary built boats for Tuppen's Outboard Marine that was a large, local retail boat store in Lake Worth. A man named Norm Goodson worked At Bud and Ron Tuppen's store. Norm, and his brother, Junior also worked for the Tuppen brothers would become key figures in Rob's future. He and Rob had been friends ever since they had learned to barefoot ski together back in Tennessee in 1957.

MASTER CRAFT BOAT NUMBER ONE RESTORED TO "FACTORY NEW CONDITION" IN 1987

Rob and his team expanded the hull of the Nautique 12 inches longer and 11 inches wider and made many other alterations to the keel line and the sides of the boat. They modeled and built in a reverse chine to the hull that made it easy to eliminate the wooden spray rails common to the earlier Nautique boats. The old boat was altered, lengthened, widened and eventually trashed once it served its purpose for creating the mold for the future of water ski boats.

Gary Brandt's fiberglass chopper gun operator went to work laying up the fiberglass mold for the hull of the prototype boat. Rob and his crew had to design and custom build the deck for the new boat from scratch. The new deck had to fit like a shoebox. They allowed one inch for shrinkage and the new deck mated up with the longer, wider hull perfectly.

As Rob and Art Cozier began rigging the new boat, they had several more decisions to make. Rudder placement was a key factor.

Also, the angle for mounting the engine and the strut that turned out to be slightly steeper than the standard 14 degrees used in other boats. Art Cozier had missed so much time away from his job at RCA that the company decided to extend Art's absence permanently by relieving him of the burden of employment so he could pursue his volunteer work of skiing and helping Rob Shirley build his boat. Rob and Flo graciously allowed Art to live with them following his substantial economic reduction and job loss.

Rob worked to rig the boat and Art worked on the interior. The resulting boat was longer, wider and weighed less than the Nautique from which it came. In early test runs their prototype rode higher in the water. The boat reached planing speed quicker and had a much smaller wake than was expected. This feature had a negative effect however, by making it harder to hold a steady and straight line as it pulled a skier through the slalom course. Rob quickly solved that problem with the addition of a second fin under the hull.

Other small changes were made to the throttle and gearshift cables by making them longer and mounting them in reverse causing them to be smoother in operation and less binding.

Rob and Art installed a large truck mirror on the dashboard in order to give the driver of the boat a panoramic view of the skier he or she would be towing through the slalom course or over the ski jump without turning around to look at the skier, and then running the risk of a collision with the ski jump or the end of the lake. The tow bar was machined out of stainless steel and Rob built a stronger support and anchoring system to keep the bar in place under heavy loads. Pulling multiple acts in a ski show or towing ski jumps for placement in tournament sites had proven to be a problem in the Nautique boats. Rob and Art decided not to use foam floatation because foam absorbs water and adds weight over time. Later boats even eliminated wooden stringers altogether.

During the construction process, several people placed orders to buy the first boats. Recently, Rob found the invoice that showed boat number two went to Wayne Grimditch. Another went to Jeff MacAnally. Rob and Art had to come up with a name for the new ski boat. There were a lot of suggestions and Rob cannot remember who came up with the name MasterCraft. Art thinks Rob should get credit for naming the boat MasterCraft. A name search of the public records indicated that the name was available...and they chose MasterCraft. At the time, a Master's rating was very popular with the American Water Ski Association and every accomplished skier, including Rob had the colorful patch jacket.

DES BURKE-KENNEDY MODELS A JACKET WITH GLOBAL PATCHES

1963 Nationals - The Allan Bromberg Memorial Trophy for the Men's National Jumping Champion awarded by Stew McDonald to Jimmy Jackson

PHOTO COURTESY OF USA WATER SKI MAGAZINE

Art Cozier trailered the boat to Canton, Ohio for the U. S. National Water Ski Championships in 1968. They were not allowed inside the grounds of the tournament so Rob and Art had the boat on display in the parking lot. It sold at that tournament.

While Rob and Art were in Canton, Ohio for the 1968 National Water Ski Championships, Rob received bad news. He had left the Ski School in the hands of one of his skiers to manage when a serious accident occurred on the ski jump and a young female skier was seriously injured that resulted in a heavy lawsuit.

As the days and weeks went by, Rob's insurance company allowed the lawsuit to drag on with ever increasing damages until finally, a meeting was held in court. The result of the meeting did not result in a settlement with the claimant being awarded compensation for her injuries. Quite the opposite happened. The judge in the case commented, "I can't believe this is happening." Unfortunately, for Rob, shortly after the sale, it almost ended his career a few days later.

Rob Shirley's insurance company filed for protection under the bankruptcy laws and avoided paying anything. Their attorney successfully pleaded for Rob's insurance company to be relieved from any liability for the lawsuit and the injury claim made by the injured skier. Rob's career as a boat builder was finished before it really got started, or so it seemed.

JIM GARDNER (ON RIGHT) BOUGHT NUMBER ONE AT THE NATIONALS IN 1968 IN OHIO AND SOLD IT BACK TO MASTER CRAFT IN 1987 IN RETURN FOR A NEW BOAT.

CHAPTER FIVE

STARTING OVER

The new boat company had not officially started up yet so Rob was able to keep his newly constructed boat molds and an old station wagon. He packed up his remaining possessions and left Florida. He drove to his grandfather's farm in Maryville, Tennessee and took up residence there.

That experience left Rob feeling down, out and depressed resulting in a period of self-imposed seclusion. He was not sure what he was going to do with the rest of his life. It was not a good time.

Rob had built a few boats for skiing friends while he was in Florida. On the strength of Rob's experience in building boats, and the fact that he retained possession of the new molds, Rob contacted Ken Merritt. Ken is an old friend who was kind enough to co-sign a loan for Rob so that he could build his first of the Master Craft Boats in the horse barn on his grandfather's farm. Ski boats would never be the same again.

After completing the boat, Rob constructed a trailer using the axle from a house trailer. He hooked up the boat to the old station wagon and headed west until he sold the boat in Nashville. He sold the first Master Craft to a man named Jim Gardner in 1968. Eventually, in 1987 Master Craft Company bought the boat back from Mr. Gardner in return for a brand new boat. The original boat was restored to pristine condition and was on display at the plant.

Rob returned to Maryville with just enough money to pay off his loan and borrow a little more money so he could build another boat.

Rob Shirley built 12 boats, one at a time and kept repeating the loan and sale process for the next two years in that old horse barn on his grandfather's farm. Sometimes it would take a couple of weeks to sell the boat. Boat dealers were reluctant to buy the boat because they had never heard of a MasterCraft Boat, and there was virtually no market for an inboard boat in 1969 that wasn't dominated by Correct Craft Boats in Orlando. There was no advertising or promotion for inboard ski boats and everyone who did not live on a lake trailered their outboard ski boats until they found a lake to ski on.

During the early years, Rob learned the valuable lesson of keeping his creditors happy by paying off his bank loans on time, or early. He built up a line of credit and it became easier to get another loan. On several occasions he had to sell a boat at a loss in order to pay off his bank loan. During those years Rob and his wife built every boat and trailer by themselves, sometime working for two days straight.

Rob made a deal with Darris Allison who had just started making Allison Craft Bass Boats. Darris would mold the parts for the MasterCraft and Rob would build and rig the boats and trailers. Darris needed the extra income and Rob needed to build boats faster.

Rob would hook up each boat trailer to his old vehicle and drive until he sold the boat and trailer, even if the trip took him all the way to California. Sometimes he sold the boat at cost in order to get back home and build another one.

In 1971, Rob met Dennis Rising. Actually, they met in Canton, Ohio when Rob was trying to sell boat number one in the parking lot of the ski club. Dennis lived on Silver Lake in Fenton, Michigan and owned a small marina called The Water Sports Marina, Inc. Dennis signed up with Rob to become his very first boat dealer. Dennis and his wife stayed with Rob and MasterCraft for 35 years.

The Marina is called Action Water Sports now, and it has new owners, and yes, they still sell MasterCraft Boats.

Rob's mission became convincing the tournament officials to use his boat to pull the three events for water ski tournaments.

Dennis recalls having dinner with Rob's dealer representative, Ken Plumlee at the old McCormick Place Exhibition Hall adjacent to Mieg's Field in downtown Chicago. Ken pulled out a napkin and handed it to Dennis and asked, "How many boats will you buy this year, Dennis?" Dennis wrote the number "80" on the napkin and that became the official sales order for 80 boats.

Both Rob and Dennis were men whose word was their bond. Rob said to Dennis, and many others, "If my word and my handshake is no good, then you can bet that my signature won't be either."

Dennis and Denise live in Marco Island, Florida now. Denise recalls sitting in the car while Dennis went in to sign the dealership agreement with Rob. "Dennis and I were on our honeymoon, and here I was in 1971 cooling my heels in a freezing car while Dennis and Rob made a deal that would give us a great life for over 35 years. We are forever grateful to Rob for providing us with the honor of being the first MasterCraft Dealer."

Rob Shirley still followed the water ski tournament circuit. But, instead of skiing in the tournaments, Rob's mission became convincing the tournament officials to use his boat to pull the three events for water ski tournaments. This became the norm at local, state and regional tournaments as the tournaments drivers, officials and skiers began to rely on Rob's boats always being available.

CHAPTER SIX

OUT OF THE ASHES

Rob came up with a new design in late 1974. Rob had always displayed the name MasterCraft boldly on the sides of all his boats. To honor the 1976 Bi-Centennial celebration, Rob came up with the now famous Stars-and-Stripes design idea. The idea worked! The first Stars-and-Stripes boats appeared in 1975.

The Stars & Stripes MasterCraft came out in 1975. Some people thought the boat was gaudy, but Rob persisted by pushing the brand and promoting the boat everywhere he could. The first good break came when MasterCraft Boats were used in several popular movies and television shows such as, Burt Reynolds in Smokey and the Bandit, and with Henry Winkler as Fonzie in the Happy Days series. The MasterCraft Boats even had a part in the hilarious comedy with Rodney Dangerfield called Caddy Shack. The big screen movie exposure was a powerful marketing tool that no amount of advertising money could buy.

Disney World in Orlando came calling. They contacted Rob at MasterCraft asking him to provide boats for their regularly scheduled water ski shows that were staged day and night with lots of lights, fanfare and fireworks.

That was when Rob came up with an innovative marketing idea. He couldn't afford to give Disney six promotional boats for free in return for the promotional exposure, so he made a deal with boat purchasers to buy the boats at a sizeable discount, subject to Disney using them for a few weeks in their shows first and then receiving their famously experienced boats after being factory refurbished.

This strategy allowed Rob the luxury of seeing the boats perform under heavy stress conditions and identifying problems. After six weeks, he would take each promotional boat back to the factory, refurbish them and correct any damages or deficiencies and then deliver the boats to the eagerly waiting purchaser.

By then, Rob had moved out of his grandfather's barn and had his own factory where he and Norm hired other employees who worked to build the growing brand of MasterCraft Boats.

A few years later, Rob built the test lake and built his home right next to the lake and in full view of the growing MasterCraft Boat Building factory.

A DISPLAY OF THE STARS & STRIPES COLLECTION OF MASTERCRAFT BOATS ARE DOCKED AT ROB'S FORMER HOME IN MARYVILLE, TENNESSEE

CHAPTER SEVEN

BILLY GARCIA

GUILLERMO "BILLY" GARCIA (1944-2015)

Also in 1974, Rob Shirley received news that Guillermo "Billy" Garcia, an internationally famous water ski champion, and member of the Mexican Team who won the Mexican National Championship 14 times and participated in 8 world tournaments, was also building boats in Mexico. Billy held a degree in electrical and mechanical engineering and had devised a few innovative ideas that impressed Rob. Billy was producing a ski boat with a growing reputation for exceptional performance. Rob travelled to Mexico to witness first-hand how Billy laid up his fiberglass boats. A very close friendship developed and Rob invited Billy and Linda to his production company in Tennessee and asked Billy to assist him in redesigning the bottom of Rob's boats.

Billy and Linda loaded up their van with the kids, Billy Boy and Monica and brought along a tricycle, a bicycle and a little red wagon propped on top and travelled to Maryville, Tennessee. The family enjoyed every minute of their stay while Billy worked with owner Rob and professional boat driver Jack Walker in designing and building a quality boat along with a motorcycle trailer and even a horse trailer. In later years, Billy' son, Billy Boy Garcia became wakeboarding champion.

THE ORIGINAL MASTER-CRAFT HORSE TRAILER

THE ORIGINAL MOTORCYCLE TRAILER ROB USED FOR HIS TRAIL BIKES

CHAPTER EIGHT

CYPRESS GARDENS

As the MasterCraft boats quickly became a legend, Rob got a call from Dick Pope, Jr., at Cypress Gardens in Winter Haven, Florida. Downing asked, "Would he be interested in providing boats for their daily water ski shows?" *** Downing or Pope asked??***

Rob was excited about providing boats for the famous attraction, but had to figure out a way to financially accomplish the job. Of course, the Gardens wanted the boats and Rob wanted the publicity they would get.

Robs friend, Billy Adams at the Maryville Bank, arranged a Small Business Administration government loan and Cypress Gardens got the boats for free. Billy Adams went on to become the head of the Tennessee Banking Commission and had a storied career that made Billy Adams a national hero for prosecuting and sending the former governor of Tennessee to prison for corruption and fraud.

Rob credits his friend for believing in him and making the growth of MasterCraft boats possible.

THE LINEUP OF MASTERCRAFT SKI SHOWBOATS AT THE
START OF THE CYPRESS GARDENS DAILY SHOWS

DICK POPE, JR., ROB SHIRLEY AND LYNN NOVAKOFSKI ON THE BEACH AT CYPRESS GARDENS

The early relationship with Dick Pope, Jr. and Cypress Gardens was a key to the success that MasterCraft Boats enjoyed. Rob spent a lot of time at the Gardens making sure the six boats performed well. Downing, as his friends and team members affectionately called Dick Pope Junior, was happy with the fuel savings that was substantial, and the fact that the boats looked so great in their shows. Downing followed his father, Dick Pope, Sr. as the President of Cypress Gardens. Other shows followed; Tommy Bartlett, Marine World USA and Water Circus were among the most famous shows acquiring the new Master Craft boats. Many ski clubs also began buying and promoting the Master Craft brand. They would often sell their boat to a club member each year and buy a fresh new one for the start of the next season.

MasterCraft became the premier towboat in more and more tournaments. In the 1974 Nationals in Seattle Washington and the 1975 National Championships in Petersburg, Virginia, MasterCraft was the official towboat and was one of the boats chosen as the official towboat after the 1977 World Championship in London, and has been pulling skiers in every World Championship since then.

CHAPTER NINE

IAN BIRDSALL
MASTERCRAFT GOES GLOBAL

Ian Birdsall was 16 years old and worked in the family garage business at the time the World Championships were held at Thorpe Park in London. Ian and his parents were all keen, self-taught recreational skiers. They had recently acquired a dealership for a small, British made inboard ski boat that they wanted to promote. They contacted the organizers of the World Water Ski tournament and signed up to occupy display space on the park grounds of the event to display their new boats. Waterskiing was popular in the South of England. The Birdsall families were Northerners, and occupying space at the prestigious world tournament was quite an accomplishment.

The Birdsall exhibit consisted of a small caravan and one of the boats floated on the water for demonstration purposes. Around the third day of the event, Ian was attending to his boat while it was beached in front of the caravan. There were no boat docks at that time. Ian and his father looked up when they heard a loud noise and saw a brashly colorful boat heading across the lake toward them. The sound of the powerful motor drowned all other noises surrounding them. It was only after the driver of the boat beached the craft that they noticed the name MasterCraft on the side of the boat. The name was totally unheard of in Europe at the time.

The driver deftly hopped over the windshield, loped across the deck and hopped down on the beach. He introduced himself to us as, "Hello, I am Rob Shirley. Would you all be so kind as to watch my boat? I have to meet up with the USA Water Ski Team."

In typical, brash Rob Shirley style and manner, he assumed even more when he asked, "Would you mind demonstrating my boat to any potential buyers?" With his marketing pitch complete, Rob simply left the keys and disappeared. Later that evening, Ian and his father loaded up their boat on its trailer and took it to the hotel where they were staying. The MasterCraft was left, unattended, in the water after dark.

Being concerned for the security of the seemingly abandoned MasterCraft, Ian and his father drove back to the lake where they hooked up the very large MasterCraft trailer to their very small European car and towed the big boat back to their hotel. The small car labored to complete the task at hand. Upon arrival at the boat ramp the next day a second MasterCraft had appeared.

It was two days further into the event before Ian and his family saw Rob Shirley again. He had been assisting the USA Water Ski Team and was also busy trying to persuade the organizers of the tournament to allow him to use his boats in the World Championship event. The Championship already had an exclusive boat sponsor. Rob's proposal would be akin to him showing up at the Masters tournament in Georgia and asking for permission to use his boat to pull men's jumping.

There is no doubt that Rob Shirley had a lot of nerve. Anyone who would ship boats 5000 miles across a vast ocean on the off chance of getting them used in a world championship that already had a boat sponsor was simply...Rob Shirley doing what a Rob Shirley does.

The Birdsall family was so impressed with Rob Shirley and his boats that he built, it wasn't hard for Rob to convince the fledgling Birdsall Boat Dealership to buy both of Rob Shirley's MasterCraft Ski boats and become an official MasterCraft Dealer, despite the fact that the Birdsall family did not have sufficient money to do so. Nor did they realize that the European people would not fall head over heels in love with the V-8 powered, 18-foot boat with the predominant stars and stripes, bedecked metal flake covered U.S. muscle boat. However, the Birdsall family signed up, and the rest of the story is history.

It took the Birdsall family 10 years to establish the MasterCraft Brand in Europe. With Rob Shirley's innovative product always being at the head of the industry, MasterCraft is now the number one towboat in International competition. The water ski industry has benefitted immensely from Rob's dedication to the sports that now make up the nine disciplines of towed related sports.

The Birdsall family credits Rob with being a true visionary who changed the face of the sport and the industry behind it.

Rob Shirley developed a friendship with Peter and Ian Birdsall in the United Kingdom and allowed them to build Master Crafts and service growing European market. It wasn't long before MasterCraft Boats had dealers in 50 European countries and a sister factory building boats in the United Kingdom. After MasterCraft was sold to the Coleman Group, Ian sold his factory to them as well and became a distributor for MasterCraft. He has since retired and can be found on the waters of the world in one of his luxury yachts. Last year Ian spent 40 weeks away from the UK visiting exotic ports of call.

Ian Birdsall sold boats in his offshore locations thereby maintaining a strong sales record when the United States market went soft, proving the strength of an international company in a slumping local economy. Ian Birdsall is now an international business consultant.

IAN BIRDSALL

IAN BIRDSALL'S MASTERCRAFT AIRPLANE

SCOTT BIRDSALL'S SPECIAL MASTERCRAFT TRUCK IN AUSTRALIA

CHAPTER TEN

THE MASTER PLAN

The 1977 edition of the MasterCraft Ski Boats were redesigned. 100 orders for new boats were taken at the Greater Miami Ski Club during the 1976 National Championships. Quoting Rob Shirley, "We were destined for success. It is just a matter of controlling costs, controlling quality and marketing, and in hiring good people."

KEN PLUMLEE, SALES MGR., CARLOS MACIEL, PROMO MGR., ROB SHIRLEY, NORM GOODSON, PLANT MGR., AND GREG DAVIS, ASST. SALES MGR.

Rob made sure he and his executive staff stayed very close to the water ski tournament scene. The main competitors to MasterCraft were the Correct Craft Ski Nautique and the Malibu Response. Correct Craft did not follow or promote the competitive very actively at that time and it was too expensive for the other manufacturers to do so. Rob traveled all over the world supporting tournaments. His competitors did not.

THE MASTER CONSULTANTS

Jack Walker was the skier's choice and a master boat driver. He was also an expert critic in the art of boat handling and performance. Rob respected Jack's expertise and sought his approval before making any changes to the MasterCraft model. If Jack said, "The steering needs to be a little tighter," or if he said, "No! This design or change won't work," that idea never made it into production.

JACK WALKER

The same expertise was available from Bob and Kris LaPoint. The brothers dominated water skiing for years and were always on top of their game. Both were generally quiet guys, but when they spoke, everyone in water skiing listened. They were a big help to Rob in the development of the shape and design of the hull of the MasterCraft in order to develop the perfect wake size and shape.

TED BARNETT

Rob remained very close to the top water skiers in the world and welcomed their opinions about what MasterCraft boats need in order for them to improve their performances. Ted Barnet was instrumental in setting up the first MasterCraft Outboard Model in 1980. His son, Leroy was a world champion slalom skier. Ted's knowledge of the Ab Crosby designed twin rig outboard was legendary. That is why the twin-rigs were the best towboats before the newly designed inboards took over.

Liz Allan
Record leap of 106' in 1966

THE CROSBY TWIN RIG
PHOTO COURTESY OF USA WATER SKI MAGAZINE

Ted would revise the control features, engine placement, prop selection and consult on weight distribution to maximize the boat performances. It was the plan for MasterCraft to become involved in the outboard boat market in order to take advantage of their popular and frequent television advertising at that time. ABC Sports televised ski tournaments and Curt Gowdy was the featured commentator.

HAM HAMBERGER

A gentleman by the name of Ham Hamberger was the former Chief Executive Officer of Mercury Outboard Motors, and later the CEO at Yamaha. Ham was a longtime friend and supporter of water skiing and the underlying technical support of the sport. Ham passed away in 2015. Because of Ham's encouragement, MasterCraft built a few boats with MercCruiser engines with Inboard/Outboard (IO) drives in order to get the IO boating industry involved in ski boats.

During that period of time when MasterCraft was the featured boat at Cypress Gardens, Chrysler Outboard Marine supplied outboard motors to the Gardens so Rob even started installing Chrysler engines in his MasterCraft Boats.

CHAPTER ELEVEN

THE MASTERCRAFT CHAMPIONS

It was Rob Shirley who came up with the idea to sponsor the athletes who were at the top of the water ski world, or had the potential to rise to the top of it. He supplied personal boats for training and practice, and even supplied financial support to help with their expenses. Some of the earlier great skiers MasterCraft sponsored included Liz Allan, Alan and Rob Kempton. Ricky McCormick, Wayne Grimditch, Sammy and Camille Duvall, Corey Pickos, Bob and Kris LaPoint, Pam Folsom, Russ Stiffler, Sally Monnier, to name just a few. MasterCraft concentrated their efforts on promoting three-event water skiing competition.

MasterCraft Boats have over 200 boats a year in circulation under sponsorship agreements, and have had for years. Very few boat companies have the resources and production capabilities to maintain sponsorship programs. But, the idea has been a productive marketing game-changer for the athletes and for MasterCraft Boats. The program will continue, and grow, especially as the towed water sports popularity increases over time.

At one time, all of the national records in all divisions of the sport were set while skiing behind a MasterCraft boat. Knee boarding, wake boarding, wake surfing, tubing, wake skating and barefoot skiing competition had not yet become popular. MasterCraft design personnel were trying to make the boat wake as small as possible. The age for the 23-foot long boats, with towers for carrying boards and for mounting loud speakers for entertaining a crowd of 10 people in order to create huge wakes, had not arrived yet.

MasterCraft supplied the ski boats to the famous show venues and also to the best skiers in the world to use for their personal training in order to promote the sport. Rob supplied over 200 boats each year as promotional boats.

THE MASTERCRAFT PRO SKI TEAM: ROW 1: RICKY McCORMICK, BRITT & TAWN LARSON, SAMMY DUVAL, JENNIFER LEACHMAN, CAMILLE DUVALL, GOEF CARRINGTON AND MARIO FOSSA. ROW 2: LUCKY LOWE, KRIS LAPOINT, CORY PICKOS, LISA SIMONEAU, BOB LAPOINT AND SCOTTY CLACK.

Rob built a fleet of outboard boats that were outfitted with 50 horsepower outboard motors that became a part of ski shows by jumping them over ski jumps and through a billowing fire. Once, a multi-boat jump boat sequence was filmed at Cypress Gardens for a movie produced by Rodney Duggar. Unfortunately, as with many good shots recorded on film, that scene did not survive the editing process and the film was left on the cutting room floor. But the sequence is memorialized on You-Tube and has been viewed by millions of people worldwide.

Rob Shirley continued to support competition water skiing with the single goal of trying to put water skiing on the global map. Water skiing made the 1972 Olympics as a Demonstration Sport in the Munich Olympics, but has never been invited in to subsequent Summer Olympic venues. However, due to the efforts of Ireland's Des Burke-Kennedy, and Switzerland's

Kuno Ritschard and the International Water Ski and Wake Board Federation (IWWF), strong bids have been made, and continue to be made for cable wake boarding, a sport that has grown beyond anyone's expectation, especially that of Rob Shirley.

In just a few years, cable-towed water sports have opened over a thousand cable parks and have the ability to tow wake boarders and water skiers in competition events without any boat whatsoever, and achieve world-class performances. Many of the parks offer a choice of cable or boat propelled skiing on separate man-made lakes that offer perfect skiing conditions all the time.

CHAPTER TWELVE

THE OLYMPIC EFFORT AND GLOBAL HISTORY

DES BURKE-KENNEDY, KUNO RITSCHARD AND THE BID TEAM AT THE OLYMPIC COMMITTEE

Contributed By Des Burke-Kennedy

Media Chairman, IWWF

It really all began in 2004.

At that time, the International Waterski & Wakeboard Federation (IWWF) was known as the IWF. Title was yet to feature Wakeboard. The challenge facing the IWWF was a significant. For many years, presenting a clear image of a Federation founded in July 1946 in Geneva, Switzerland, with so many disciplines involved, was beyond the reach of those involved. The solution was created in the shape of the Waterski & Wakeboard World Cup Series. This was to be a single consistent marketing brand.

The concept was to create an annual calendar of significant cash prize events under the World Cup banner. Each World Cup Stop would contain at least two IWWF disciplines. Initially, Slalom, Tricks and Jump were chosen. Only the top 20 IWWF highest ranked athletes would qualify for invitation to guarantee quality. The aim for the venues was to go "Down Town" to capture the biggest possible audiences to generate the widest appeal for TV and sponsors.

So much for the plan. Now the nuts and bolts had to be added. Finding a boat provider was one of the first challenges. Could any manufacturer deliver boats to the far corners of the earth? Since this was to be a high quality-marketing project, the hope was that a high quality boat could be sourced.

Just before Christmas 2003, IWWF President Kuno Ritschard, IWWF and Marketing & Media Chairman Des Burke-Kennedy, flew to London to meet MasterCraft Europe chief Ian Birdsall. What emerged from that eventful day was a unique and history making agreement between MasterCraft and IWWF. This involved the provision of two boats for every World Cup Stop. Little did we know that this was to create something never before achieved in our sport on such a scale!

At the time of writing, a total of 45 World Cup Stops have been successfully completed around the globe. The event has paid out close to $6 million in cash prizes to our athletes. Our TV media distribution partner, IMG have a worldwide sales force in 30 regional offices and a home reach of 712 million via 68 Broadcasters in three TV Magazine shows. A recent World Cup Stop achieved over 700 hours of airing time through 2,500 transmissions. This delivered an estimated media value of $5 million for the recent World Cup Stop in Mandurah, Western Australia.

As World Cup partners, the IWWF and MasterCraft brought the event to very large audiences at some very exotic venues which included France, Great Britain, Russia, China, Singapore, Qatar, Northern Ireland, Egypt, Malaysia, South Korea, Borneo, Japan and Indonesia. Over 3 million Press Releases were delivered along the way to generate interest - and to help make the MasterCraft brand a truly global one.

IWWF PRO TOUR IN PARIS

IWWF Pro Tour in Russia

IWWF Pro Tour in Malaysia

IWWF PRO TOUR IN SINGAPORE

WORLD CUP TOUR IN KOREA 2015

WORLD CUP TOUR IN IRELAND 2015

WORLD CUP TOUR IN QATAR 2015

A MasterCraft full of Judges and Officials in China 2015

CHAPTER THIRTEEN

LUXURY SKI BOATS

MasterCraft Boats entered the luxury boat market in the most unlikely manner. Rob Shirley was embarrassed into it by his banker who simply wanted to buy a boat for his new lake home in Tennessee. Rob was called from his office one day to show his old friend through the MasterCraft Factory on a personally guided tour. He showed his old friend through the plant, proudly pointing out the newest line of ski boats, features, molds, construction and Rob's custom processes. He took his banker through the skier's photo gallery where Rob bragged about the world and national champion skiers who were using MasterCraft boats and breaking records behind them. With his chest bursting with pride, Rob outlined the marketing plan for the future and bragged about the successes his creation already had achieved.

After his guest left the factory, Rob basked in the glow of having impressed his friend, Billy Adams, the president of the Bank of Maryville, the man who had loaned Rob the money for all of his financial needs over the years.

Rob was shocked when he received a phone call from Billy Adams' assistant at the bank the very next day.

"Why were you not willing to sell my boss a boat when he visited your factory yesterday?"

"What do you mean?" Rob replied. "You told Billy Adams that you built boats for water skiers and he took your comment to mean that in order for him to get one of your boats he had to be a tournament water skier."

"I'll call Billy myself and take care of that misconception immediately," Rob replied. "I had no idea that Billy wanted to buy one." A few weeks later the first luxury outfitted MasterCraft Ski Boat was moored at the dock owned by the president of The Bank of Maryville, Tennessee. Billy was a huge help to MasterCraft and the Shirley's during the struggling years. It was the least he could do, and it turned into a huge marketing success.

ROB SHIRLEY FOUNDER OF MASTERCRAFT

The boat dealers who ordered MasterCraft boats in the past only purchased boats when they had a paying customer lined up to buy one. With the luxuriously outfitted MasterCraft boat, they now had a boat that adorned their showroom floors, could be a show stopper at the boat shows, and satisfy the needs and wants of the recreational skier that wanted a luxury version of the boats they had seen on television or at Cypress Gardens. In the early eighties the dealers were fighting for a protected territory and ordering MasterCraft boats by the truckload.

The non-serious skier turned out to be a serious buyer who just wanted something special sitting on the trailer in his yard or floating next to his boat dock at the lake cottage he used on weekends. Rob produced more boats than ever.

Denny Rising from Water Sports Marine in Fenton, Michigan was the first dealer to sell over 100 boats a year. Jim Andrews of JOA Marine in Atlanta, Georgia hit 100 sales, while other dealers even got bigger. These dealers opened up Rob's eyes to paying more attention to the creature comforts of color, upholstery, carpet and optional graphics. Rob had learned to pay attention to the wives who often were the actual purchasers, or a partner of the purchase to begin with. What she had to say was important in every sale.

Rob also started paying more attention to the children of the skiing family. Youngsters who were competitive skiers would often tell their parents, "I want a MasterCraft Boat." Rob began to realize that when a child becomes an adult, he also becomes the potential purchaser of a boat on his own.

MasterCraft Boats sponsored a scholarship in the name of Jimmy McCormick, a youngster that was fatally injured and later died as a result of a jumping accident at his father's ski school in Florida. Jimmy McCormick was the nephew of World Champion Ricky McCormick. Jim and Ricky waved the flag for MasterCraft Boats for many years.

MasterCraft Boats had the smallest wake and became the skier's choice, especially when the skier was given the option of several boat choices available. MasterCraft sponsored many ski schools around the country; some of them even received a free boat. The children who were the skiers were often the influencing factor in the parent's decision of what kind of ski boat to buy.

MasterCraft, under Rob Shirley's direction, began providing Promotional Boats to individuals who agreed to take the boat to a specific number of tournaments in his region. The theory was that the tournaments became more professional and the skiers began to anticipate better boats to be used at each and every tournament site.

The practice of providing promotional boats to dedicated individuals in the sport became a standard practice for MasterCraft and Correct Craft Boats. They were the only ones who had the sales volume and could afford to do that. Currently, MasterCraft has over 200 promotional boats in circulation for water skiers, wake boarders and wake surfing competitors at the elite levels.

The two-edged sword of the promotion deal specified that the owner of the boat attend as many as 10 tournaments and make his boat available to pull any or all of the skiing events. At the end of the season the owner could sell the boat at a significant profit and make a deal for another new boat on the same plan. Rob's friend, Bill Caldwell made that huge sacrifice, as did many others by taking their MasterCraft boats to 20 or more local, regional and national tournaments in order to get the boat at a tremendous discount. Most of the Promotional boat owners had someone lined up to buy their well-used, but impeccably maintained MasterCraft boat. During the height of the promo program, several boats would arrive at the tournament site as a backup and some of them were hardly ever used.

Two of the longest standing members of the MasterCraft promotional team were Ken Plumlee and Stan and Donna Switzer who worked tirelessly to promote MasterCraft boats for many years.

Other boat manufacturing companies began to notice the popularity and the volume of business MasterCraft and Correct Craft were doing. They tried to compete by building a similar boat but fell short when they realized how much time and expertise it took to build a special boat, or how much money it cost to support an entire sport.

 But, to build a credible boat that performs with regularity, day in and day out at tournaments, and pulling four-tiered pyramids and other heavy loads in ski shows every day is a commitment to quality and dedication, and MasterCraft boats handled the task beautifully.

Rob had to hire a special person to manage the promo boat program. That special person was Gary Mahler who took the job very seriously and made it a model program for all other companies who were offering promotion boats.

Gary was also in charge of testing boats, and in 1980 Rob built his own test lake that became a huge asset and saved the company thousands of dollars when they stopped trailering boats to a lake for testing them that was 10 miles away.

Other employees to whom Rob owes a special debt of gratitude and loyalty was Cotton Welshan who stayed with the company for 35 years. Another man, Glen Tinker was a master model maker and became the man who made, built and perfected the molds. He was a special friend and will be missed forever. Rest in peace, Glen. Rob entrusted the production of MasterCraft Boats to Norm Goodson. Norm developed the boat building industry's first production line where workers on the line did repeated tasks over and over again as the boat hulls moved past them on a special track. They repeated their job five times a day. Even the truck drivers who delivered the MasterCraft Boats were proud to be seen with a load of six boats as they traveled across the country. It was a moving billboard and MasterCraft had its own fleet of trucks and drivers who kept them looking pristine. Pride was in huge supply around the MasterCraft Factory.

Eventually, Rob handed off the daily contact with the boat dealers around the country to Ken Plumlee. Everyone who did business with Ken enjoyed a special brand of personal attention and they prospered, flourished and enjoyed the experience because of Ken. He was a key employee that made it possible for Rob to become heavily involved in marketing and promotion after 1978.

CHAPTER FOURTEEN

JIM AND LANCE SMITH

MasterCraft Boat Company owned a Cessna 421 aircraft and employed a full time pilot to fly it. If Rob's schedule called for him to see two different dealers in two different cities in one day, it was easy to do. Should a customer have a problem and needed a technician from the factory to solve that problem, it was also easy to accomplish. MasterCraft sales were booming and the company was growing. Nobody in the industry had yet considered using an airplane to support his or her business activities. During the ski tournament season, the plane was in constant use by shuttling Rob between scheduled events that happened on the same day, such as a tournament or a boat show.

Rob tells the story of Jim Smith, a firefighter in Long Beach, California. Jim's schedule called for one month on duty and one month off. He traveled with Rob to Saudi Arabia to set up a MasterCraft Dealer there. Jim was highly skilled in graphic design and created the first MasterCraft Parts Catalogue. Jim died way too early. Rob still mourns the loss of his friend. But the opportunity to lessen the mourning period for Jim's son, Lance came up. Lance is the same age as Rob's son, Mike. Rob was a good friend of King Hussein of Jordan, and he is even a better friend to King Abdulla. Rob contacted another friend who was in charge of the King's Marine Facilities and arranged for Lance to have a job at the palace teaching water skiing and scuba diving to the King's children. Lance lived at the Royal Palace for two years.

KING HUSSEIN OF JORDAN OFTEN VISITED CYPRESS GARDENS

THE KING PREPARING TO SKI BEHIND A MASTERCRAFT OUTBOARD, HIS BIRTHDAY GIFT, A
MASTERCRAFT BY LEBANESE WORLD CHAMPION, SIMON KHOURY

When Lance left Jordan he returned to Las Vegas as an active firefighter, got married and has two children. Rob Shirley is pretty sure that Lance's father would have been pleased with the help his son got from Rob.

LANCE AND JILL SMITH AND THE BOYS

Rob Shirley remembers with pleasure the day he hired Randy Freeman who eventually became Rob's plant manager. He watched Randy while he worked at a gas station and was amazed at how he handled the customers who came to the station. Rob asked Randy, "How would you like to come work for me at the boat factory?"

Rob remembers his reply to this very day. "What would I do?" asked Randy. Rob's reply was equally vague. He said, "I'm not sure, but I want you with my company." Back in those early days in Blount County, Tennessee there were no building codes, no OSHA, and nobody to tell Rob what to do or how to do it. So, they built a factory and produced five boats a day with a staff of 100 employees. There was no sprinkler system. Sprinklers wouldn't put out a fiberglass fire anyway. The boating industry is littered with the ashes of many fiberglass fires. Only a foam machine would work if the airport fire department could get to the building in time. Most of them don't unless the building that is burning is located at an airport. Randy Freeman was one of the special men who contributed much. Rob and Randy's friendship is still solid these many years later.

CHAPTER FIFTEEN

LESLIE "SKIP" GILKERSON

THE PRO SKI TOUR

Rob Shirley bumped heads with the leaders of AWSA (American Water Ski Association) at that time when he set out to create and sponsor the Professional Water Ski Tour. AWSA Officials had the mistaken idea that professional skiing would hinder getting water skiing into the Olympics as a regular event. Water skiing was an exhibition sport at the 1972 Olympics in Munich. It has not yet returned in any capacity to any subsequent Olympic Games, in part because it required a mechanical means of propulsion; namely, the towboat.

The Pro Tour, led by Rob Shirley and MasterCraft Boats secured sponsorships from Ford Motor Company, Coors Brewing Company, Mercury and Yamaha Outboard Motors and most other popular brands of water skiing equipment that joined in with financial help and access to sponsored television shows.

With or without USA Water Ski Association, Rob needed a very special man to set up and run all of the pro tour events and make sure all the equipment and ski sites were properly set up. Rob recruited a former Cypress Gardens and Tommy Bartlett show skier, Skip Gilkerson. Skip had also run the pro snow skiing tour in Aspen, Colorado. He could not have picked a better man for the job.

SKIP GILKERSON ON SHOE SKIS IN TOMMY BARTLETT'S WISCONSIN DELLS SHOWS

Under Skip's leadership, the pro water ski tour awarded cash prizes to the winners and helped them with their expenses. Judges and officials were also paid which had never been done before. One of the long-term benefits of the pro ski tour was the sale of refurbished boats that had been used to train skiers and pull skiers in various tournaments all over the world.

In the summer of 1959, three members of the Cypress Gardens water ski show team came to Indiana Beach at the request of Tom Spackman, the owner of the resort. Their mission was to teach local Monticello, Indiana skiers to water ski well enough to put on ski shows every day at Indiana Beach Resort. Jerry Imber, Florence Cloud and Jon Broderick spent two weeks at Indiana Beach while on vacation from the Cypress Gardens water ski shows at the Water Ski Capitol of the world at that time.

The result was that Indiana Beach Ski Shows became the summertime featured daily performances lasting over 50 years. In that first two-weeks, Skip Gilkerson was recruited from the lifeguard staff along with his sister, Judes Gilkerson, Gary Boomershine, Joy Spackman and several others. Two weeks later, a full-blown water ski show was on the water at Lake Shaffer.

**SKIP AND JUDES GILKERSON WERE STARS IN TOMMY BARTLETT'S
SKI SHOWS AT THE WISCONSIN DELLS**

After the season ending Labor Day show, Jerry and Jon invited Skip to Cypress Gardens for a tryout. Skip promised his father that he would return home to finish college in return for following his water skiing dream for a while. Skip kept his promise to his father by not only getting his college degree, he also completed a Master's Degree later in life.

While waiting in the ski room to take the mandatory medical exam for all Gardens employees, Skip was drafted into the clown act for the morning show. He was ordered to do the "slide" up the jump on his belly in the clown act called Water Ski Baseball. On skis with no heel binders, behind the big Correct Craft boats with powerful Chrysler engines and huge wakes, Skip made his first appearance as a Cypress Gardens Skier.

Later, that same day, Jerry Imber gave Skip his jumper skis and his own locker in the ski room and retired from the show to become one of Cypress Garden's best photographers of water skiing.

JERRY IMBER &
MARY LOU RHODES
AT CYPRESS GAR-
DENS IN 1959

JON BRODERICK AND HIS AQUA FOLLIES SKI MACHINE, CAPE CORAL, FLORIDA 1971-1981, TOWNSEND, TN AND SAN ANTONIO, TX.

Skip's career at Cypress Gardens was exciting, full of drama and ended shortly after he won the Dixie slalom championship in the three event annual tournament in April 1960. He was the first skier out when the men's event began. Skip was an enthusiastic slalom skier that struggled to make 30 miles per hour on a long line. But, right after he finished his run, the wind blew, the rains came and the slalom course for all other skiers, including world champion Joe

Cash, was too rough to see the buoys, much less ski around them. In the end, Skip Gilkerson was second of the two men to complete a pass at any speed, and he came in second to Philippe Logut, 1959 World Trick Skiing Champion of France.

That same night at the formal party in the Cypress Gardens dining room, Skip, being "Skip," showed up in a formal tuxedo emulating the same costume worn by Stu McDonald, the famous water ski judge, skier and ABC Sports commentator from Wide World of Sports. Like Stu, Skip wore no shoes. After presenting Skip with his 2nd place trophy for the Dixie Slalom event, Dick Pope, Jr. invited Skip to leave the Gardens and find employment elsewhere.

The next summer, and for many years after that, Skip was a featured performer at the Wisconsin Dells in the Tommy Bartlett Ski Shows, and eventually ski became the show director. He was the man that hired Rob Shirley as a skier in the Bartlett Show the summer Rob turned his ski school over to someone else to run while he was gone.

In the winters, Skip wore several hats. He became a member of the Aspen Snow Ski Patrol. He finished college. He became a teacher, a coach bodybuilder and even organized the Pro Ski Events in Aspen, Colorado.

The sun was setting on Skip's show skiing career when, in 1985, he got a call from Rob Shirley at Skip's home in Winter Haven, Florida. Rob had an idea he wanted Skip to listen to and they met for lunch at the old Cypress Gardens Sheraton Inn. They talked for four hours. Anyone who knows Skip, knows that conversations can last a while; but this time it was Rob Shirley, the CEO and President of MasterCraft Boats who was doing the talking.

Skip was hired to organize, set up and run the Professional Water Ski Tour that Master-Craft Boats wanted to sponsor. They agreed to a two-year contract that gave Skip the time he needed to do the job. Rob never did buy Skip lunch that day. Instead, he gave Skip the Master-Craft Company position and sent him off to Ocho Rios, Jamaica where the first pro water ski event was due to start the next few days. Skip was ordered to fly first class, and to this very day, Skip gives Rob Shirley all the credit for always doing things in a first class manner.

Skip, when asked, "What kind of a boss was Rob Shirley?" He replied, "Rob expected me to do the job that I was hired to do. He did not interfere, micro-manage or even make suggestions. He was a *no nonsense* perfectionist that did not give praise very often. He expected perfection and results and paid a generous wage to get them."

Skip tells the story about the struggling water ski pro tour having only four events in 1986. Revenues were low and the tour was in trouble. Rob called Skip into his office. "I just knew that I was going to be fired, laid off or reassigned," Skip recalled. "But, from Rob, one should always expect the unexpected." Rob was going over the figures from the first four events conducted on the tour.

"We have to spend money in order to make money, Skip. Here, take the company credit card and go set up 8 events this year. Spare no expense and do it right when you go to West Palm Beach." Skiers remember when the pro tour doubled its efforts and began to make a significant impact.

On one particular trip with the motor home that Skip used to pull boats and go to different events, the motor home suffered a major breakdown. Skip was just sure he was going to suffer the wrath of his boss when he called to report the breakdown. Instead, he got the unexpected. "Get it fixed and pay whatever you have to get it done quickly," Rob informed him. Rob knew better than anyone else, that accidents happen when you least expect them. Four days later, Skip was on the road again.

Skip recalls being at one National Championship event when MasterCraft was the recipient of an unlucky draw during the towboat selection, and none of the MasterCraft boats were going to be used in any of the televised final events. Skip reported this fact to Rob. Rob ordered all MasterCraft boats to be pulled out of the water and removed from the site of the tournament immediately. Skip issued the order and the boats were loaded onto the trailers. The tournament director went berserk with panic as the boats were being loaded. Needless to say, new towing assignments were issued and MasterCraft pulled its fair share of the final skiing events.

Skip stayed with MasterCraft for 20 years, retiring after the sale of the company to Coleman Industries. In recapping his water ski career, Skip says, "I was the luckiest guy in the world to be able to perform in the Bartlett shows at the Dells and entertain thousands of people. I know I wasn't the greatest skier that ever lived, but I was always the most enthusiastic. I put all I had into every act. I hope the people who saw me ski enjoyed it just half as much as I did, because I loved every minute of performing."

Skip continued as if there were more to the story, and there was. "Just when I thought it was over, Rob Shirley came into my life on a white horse and offered me an even greater job than I had before."

Skip Gilkerson has made an impact on water skiing that outweighs his contributions to show skiing on the water. The pro ski tour was a great marketing tool. Twenty million viewers tuned in to watch the televised events regularly. Freestyle skiing was added to the pro tour event with world class show skiers now being able to compete in special jumping events where distance did not matter as much as the form, difficulty and style of the tricks performed in the air while flying off the ramp. Skiers like Scotty Clack and Shellie Blum became famous, as did many others in this very popular and watchable event. Shellie has published a book on her accomplishments, and serious injuries. That book is available through Barnes & Noble.

GARRY STOUT AND SKIP WITH MARK JACKSON
AT THE 2015 WORLD SHOW SKIING CHAMPIONSHIPS
SKIP SERVED AS A JUDGE. MARK COMMENTATED ON THE LIVE STREAM TV COVERAGE

And just when you think you have heard it all, Skip adds…"Let me tell you about my niece and nephews. They are my sister's children, Judy (Judes) Gilkerson-May."

He infected the sport with an endless dose of his own character, enthusiasm and love of the sport that will survive him for generations to come. Skip never had any children of his own, but he had a hand in training his nephew, Mathew May to be an exceptional show skier and international champion now living in Australia. Matt's older brother, although not an active skier, was the editor of Water Ski Magazine for years, and Amy, Skips niece is still on the staff of The Golf Channel, the popular Orlando based TV station that broadcasts golfing news on cable television worldwide.

Under Skip's guidance, Matt skied in his first ski show at the age of one. By 14 he was competing on the Pro Tour. He was National Barefoot Jumping Champion and holder of the Boy's Division record. By the time he turned 15, Matt was in the Finals in Freestyle Jumping, and made the finals in the X-Games in barefooting. He later went on to Rollins College where he was named to the All American Team. Matt now lives in Australia where he twice won the National Championship and set records in jumping.

Judes spent her entire ski career and later, her professional life at The Wisconsin Dells where she now manages the food services operation. Matt grew up on Lake Delton where his famous Uncle coached him every day.

SKIP AND JUDES GILKERSON WITH NEPHEW MATT MAY,

MATT MAY AND UNCLE SKIP GILKERSON ON LAKE DELTON

Skip's induction into the USA Water Ski Hall Of Fame symbolizes the thanks and appreciation for his contributions to the sport of water skiing. World famous photographer and former Cypress Gardens ski show director Lynn Novakofski said it best; "The trophy for the best show skier every year at the National Show Skiing Tournament ought to be called the Annual Skip Gilkerson Award."

SKIP REFLECTING ON HIS PORTRAIT AT THE USA WATER SKI MUSEUM AND HALL OF FAME WHERE HIS ACCOMPLISHMENTS EXTEND BEYOND THE SHOW SKI CIRCLE AT THE WISCONSIN DELLS.

And it is... only now, it must be given posthumously. On October 7, 2015 Skip was on his way to a practice session with his San Marcos High School

Swim Team for an early morning workout. He was riding his motorcycle when he swerved to avoid hitting a deer that was crossing the highway. The bike went down and skidded into the opposite lane when suddenly, a truck headed in the opposite direction could not avoid hitting Skip causing massive injuries. Skip survived many of the surgical procedures doctors performed in order to try to save his life. Nurses said, "It is a miracle he is still with us." But, even the strongest of men, including Skip, could not recover from those injuries. On October 25, 2015, while listening to John Denver's music, Skip Gilkerson passed away.

A memorial service was held in New Braunfels, Texas and many of Skip's friends from all over the world attended. They ran, walked or rode bikes over Skip's favorite place next to the Guadalupe River, and cheered for his favorite team, the Green Bay Packers the next day at the Texas Ski Ranch.

MasterCraft Boat Company led the way in raising money to help Sharon Gilkerson with the monumental hospital bills. San Marcos High School honored their favorite "Coach Skip" by

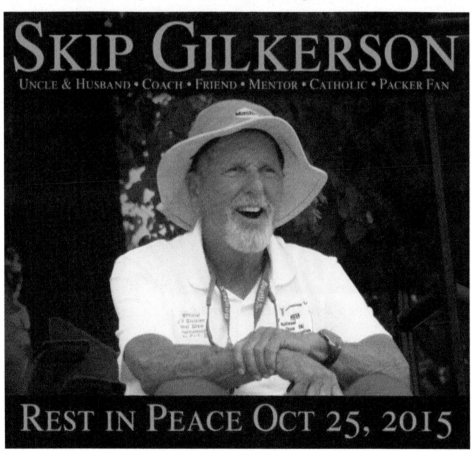

placing his initials on their helmets, and then proceeded to qualify for the State Football Championship Tournament.

CHAPTER SIXTEEN

FRED HARDWICK

FRED AND NANCY HARDWICK

Fred Hardwick met Rob Shirley in 1968 at a waterski tournament in Florida. Rob had just started MasterCraft Boat Company and was taking his new and innovative product around to tournaments for exposure. The boat was wider and lighter than anything that had been seen

in the water skiing and ski boat industry before. The spray that used to interfere with the skiers was low and seemingly nonexistent. The size and shape of new boat wakes were small and soft. Rob was an innovator and marketer with a keen entrepreneurial high-strung spirit. Fred immediately admired and liked him.

FRED, SKIP AND NANCY HARDWICK

Fred was never a great water skier. He won a few National medals and had his moments but was always a few buoys short in the slalom event, a few feet shorter than the competition in jumping and several trick skiing points short of being one of the really great ones. In 1971, Fred moved over from competition skiing to show skiing in part to help pay his way through college. In 1975, Fred Hardwick started graduate school that was the beginning of a major turn in his life. Fred went to school on a Research Fellowship as a Graduate Assistant and was assigned to work for Professor Dr. William P. Lloyd. Fred's thesis was built around a water ski show that he had directed at EXPO 75 in Okinawa, Japan. The thesis project followed the bidding, contract negotiations, operations and final results of the international operation. Dr. Lloyd loved the project and eventually partnered with Tommy Bartlett and Fred to build a water ski show in the Smoky Mountains of east Tennessee. Tommy was the marketer, Dr. Lloyd was the financial partner and Fred was the operator. In 1978, Fred opened the Tommy Bartlett Ski, Sky & Stage Show in Pigeon Forge, Tennessee.

POSTER FROM THE TOMMY BARTLETT WATER CIRCUS

The show was just 35 miles from Maryville, Tennessee where Rob Shirley was in full swing with MasterCraft Boat Company. MasterCraft sponsored Fred's show with both traditional towboats and "jump boats." It was the beginning of a lifetime friendship between Rob Shirley and Fred Hardwick.

THE MASTERCRAFT JUMP BOATS WERE FEATURED IN THE TOMMY BARTLETT SKI SHOWS AT THE WISCONSIN DELLS AND IN THE SKI SHOW IN PIGEON FORGE, TENNESSEE

In 1982, Dr. Lloyd and Fred bought Tommy Bartlett's ownership share in the Tennessee operation and formed a new venture we called, "Water Ski Shows, Inc." Over the next decade they expanded the water ski shows over six continents. They produced water ski and live stunt shows for theme parks and expositions around the world. From the Six Flags Parks to the Indiana Beach Resort in Monticello, Indiana USA, to the Expo 88 in Australia to Holiday Park in Europe and dozens of shows and parks in between. Fred's company shows were on six of the seven continents and MasterCraft provided the boats for all of them. They expanded into movies with Smoky and the Bandit, Water World and the James Bond series. By this time, Rob Shirley had expanded his MasterCraft brand into water skis as well as boats and he supported Fred with both products in all their shows.

THE MASTERCRAFT CAR/BOAT IN PIGEON FORGE, TN

In 1987, Fred met Dolly Parton and together they launched into another entertainment business called the Dixie Stampede Dinner Attraction. It was an immediate hit and the concept now feeds and entertains nearly 2 million visitors annually with locations in Pigeon Forge, Tennessee; Branson, Missouri and Myrtle Beach, South Carolina. The operations were such a big hit that they sold Water Ski Shows, Inc. to the employees in 1995 to give Fred more time with the booming dinner attractions. Fred financed the sale to them over 10 years. The skiers paid Fred back in three.

Rob and Fred's friendship continued to grow through their mutual love of off road motorcycle riding. They started riding together in 1977. Rob talked Fred into buying his first dirt bike. They never stopped riding. Fred's son, Ryan got his first motorcycle when he was two years old. Thirty-three years later, he is still riding with both Rob and his Dad. Their riding adventures included National Enduros and exotic Adventure Rides that Rob created.

There were some bruises along the way. In 1988, Rob got Fred out of the woods in Michigan with two broken legs and flew him in his private plane to a hospital in Tennessee. Everything turned out well.

Ryan Hardwick started "Mountain Motorsports" and is now one of the largest purveyors of motorcycles and personal watercraft in the world with eight locations spreading around Atlanta, Georgia and east Tennessee.

Fred Hardwick has enjoyed enormous success in the water skiing and theme park entertainment business. In his words, it is, "All because of one man, Rob Shirley! He has been a lifetime inspiration, teacher, coach, marketer, financier, supporter and most of all, best friend."

CHAPTER SEVENTEEN

RANDY FREEMAN

In the early 1980's, Randy Freeman was 22 years old, fresh out of college, just married with a passion for water skiing and mechanics, especially automotive. Winter Haven, Florida was his home and hanging out with friends at Cypress Gardens and water skiing occupied most of his time when Randy's life abruptly changed.

He met Rob Shirley.

"Rob began by trusting me with a few tasks and projects, especially automotive and mechanical," Randy recalled. It was the beginning of a lifelong friendship, an adventure and a career. About a month after Randy met Rob, he received a phone call. The message was always the same.

"What are you doing?" Rob always asked the same question. But, this one was different. It wasn't a question about one of his cars, or motorcycles, or about the boats he was building with Jack Walker. It was about coming to work for Rob at the MasterCraft plant in Maryville, Tennessee.

"Whoa!"

That question came at Randy from left field. Rob asked him to accept a position as purchasing agent at the MasterCraft Plant. Randy knew nothing about boatbuilding and had no clue about what a purchasing agent did. But, Rob Shirley was convincing, persuasive and absolutely trustworthy, even when he was wrong, which was not often.

Randy and his new bride decided to visit Maryville, Tennessee and check out Rob's offer. They had no preconceived notion and had no experience in forming one. They trusted Rob completely, and that trust has never wavered in the course of what was to become his entire career and lifetime relationship with Rob Shirley.

Rob picked Randy and his new bride up at the Winter Haven Airport in April that year. Both Randy and his wife were wearing Bermuda shorts suitable for a Florida spring day. When they arrived in Maryville a few hours later, it was cold up in the Smokey Mountains and traces of snow were still on the ground.

RANDY AND MALIEAH FREEMAN

Randy, and the new Mrs. Freeman, not only survived the trip and the cold weather, they stayed in Maryville for a memorable career, and for a lifetime of adventures, one after another...gathering albums full of memories that included having Rob Shirley as a best friend and mentor.

"Needless to say, Rob easily talked me into the job at MasterCraft," Randy recalled. "I knew nothing about purchasing, but trusted Rob when he told me not to worry, that everyone at MasterCraft helps everyone else out. He was right. Thanks to Steve Blair, our warehouse supervisor, I picked up the details of my job pretty quick."

Rob persistently taught Randy the ropes and he learned quickly what was expected. Rob asked questions that Randy did not have the answers to, and by the time Rob asked the question a second time, Randy had the answer. He learned, and remembered who supplied a part, how much it cost, how many they had on hand, and when the next shipment was coming in. In the pre-computer days, MasterCraft used the traditional green card system that required memorization and organization.

Once Randy became proficient at his position, Rob relaxed the mentoring pressure and their true friendship began. Randy was invited to go on a motorcycle trail ride with Rob. Randy had ridden motorcycles as a youngster, but he was not prepared for the abuse a trail ride with Rob did to one's body. Randy loved every painful minute of the ride, even though he could barely get around with his abused body for the following few days.

"Rob laughed his head off at my wounded and bruised body," Randy recalled. "But it was the start of a lifelong friendship that has lasted to this very day."

Randy and Rob had a blast as they enjoyed time away from work. It never hurt that Randy could also fix anything that they broke during the trail rides before the next adventure came around for them to tear up something else. Each time they shared an adventure, Rob and Randy solved the world problems and consulted together on the MasterCraft plant issues. They conjured up new projects as they continued the happy abuse they suffered on the trails, wherever those trails went.

Randy became an innovator, a leader and a responsible and extremely competent worker, always striving to take every challenge to the next level, whether it was good, bad or ugly. Rob soon promoted Randy to assistant plant manager where he continued mentoring under another great man, Norm Goodson. From Norm, Randy learned to run a production facility, lead people and grow respect without having to command it. As events followed their logical progression, Randy was later promoted to plant manager and Norm took on the responsibility of research, development and engineering.

It was during the mid 1980's when Rob sold MasterCraft to the Coleman family. That was a very scary time for Randy until Rob came down to his office to share his plan for the future of MasterCraft Boats. Rob assured Randy that he had the utmost confidence and that Randy shouldn't worry. He would grow through experience and that his life would be better than Rob could ever offer him personally. As the history of MasterCraft unfolded in the post Rob Shirley years, the future turned out to be great for the Freeman Family just as Rob Shirley promised that it would. Rob had never broken a promise to Randy Freeman. Once the pressure was off and the tension of the transfer of ownership lessened, MasterCraft flourished. Everything was truly better for all of the employees of the company. MasterCraft built better boats. Exceptional MasterCraft employees became even better, and Mr. Coleman gave the respect they had from Rob in even greater measure. The plant developed newer products under Rob's direction and working at MasterCraft was more fun than ever.

From the beginning, Rob, Randy, and his circle of MasterCraft folks became lifelong friends. To this day, they still vacation annually as a family and have laughs that are far beyond what Randy feels that they deserve. Randy gives all the thanks to Rob. One adventure with Rob is not trumped by any other adventure. But without a doubt, there were times that Randy wasn't sure they were going to get out without serious injury, or at all. Randy proudly states, "When it was all said and done, it was truly so much fun that I would do it again, knowing I was in for the journey. We ran the rapids of raging rivers during peak flood conditions with no clue of what we were doing. We rode into no-man's land with no maps or food, and only the vague hint that he felt we could come out where we could revive ourselves and go again. Rob left Randy while he singlehandedly fought a fiberglass fire in a dumpster at the plant with a garden hose while Rob was on the phone. Of course, that was before cell phones were common. Rob still tries to deny that one! We've slept in old mining shacks with below freezing temperatures at 13,000 ft. elevations while deep into bear country, and visited native villages in Central America while riding in hand-carved canoes in piranha infested rivers. You name it, and we quite possibly made an adventure out of it.

Randy proudly said, "Life is good with friends who see you for who you really are and love and respect you anyway. Rob is a natural born motivator and his acute judge of character is uncanny." Randy considers Rob a true lifelong friend.

"He's an ok dude too," Randy says. "Thank you so very much for everything, from 1981 to today. If it hadn't been for his confidence and trust, the Freeman family would not be what it is today." Randy's wife and boys all love and respect Rob. He has a paragraph in every chapter of their lives.

CHAPTER EIGHTEEN

GARY MAHLER

GARY MAHLER, ANOTHER MEMBER OF THE MASTERCRAFT LONG LIST OF WATER SKI
HALL OF FAME MEMBERS WHOSE CAREERS WERE INFLUENCED
BY ROB SHIRLEY AND MASTERCRAFT BOATS

Gary Mahler grew up water skiing behind a 13-foot Boston Whaler on the intercostal waterway in Florida. He knew there had to be a better ski boat somewhere. Someone must have designed a special purpose boat just for water skiing.

That person was Rob Shirley. He was somewhat a local celebrity that ran a popular ski school on Lake Osborne in Lake Worth, Florida. Rob was also a member of the Ski Club of The Palm Beaches and served as their President. Gary didn't know Rob at that time, but he was well known to the local skiers on Lake Osborne and Lake Ida, which were the current hot beds for year-round skiing.

Gary sold his Boston Whaler and went to Tuppens Marina in Lake Worth to look at the new MasterCraft ski boat Tuppens had on display. He had seen one while driving up US 1. Although he couldn't afford a new boat, he was able to buy a used 1973 MasterCraft from Alan Kempton, a world champion skier from Tampa. It was a great boat and he was hooked!

It was in the spring of 1976 when Rob Shirley came down to Lake Ida in Delray Beach to test a new hull design. Rob had borrowed Tom McCord's boat that he had made wider and longer. That eventual design became a new 19' MasterCraft boat that became an industry game- changer. Gary remembered seeing that boat during an exhibition at the 1976 Nationals and could not believe that a boat that long could turn better and have a smaller wake. It just didn't make sense to Gary at the time, but it was true.

Gary had attended New England College in New Hampshire as a business and marketing Major. NEC offered internship programs during the spring semester for seniors provided you completed the graduation requirements. Gary wrote a letter to MasterCraft Boat Company asking Rob for an internship. Rob replied, saying he needed a promotional coordinator to oversee where his tournament boats were going to be each weekend. Gary took the job.

Gary drove to Maryville, Tennessee. He got rear ended in an auto accident on the way during an ice storm and arrived with my damaged van and a dirt bike.

That is how Gary's relationship with Rob started in 1979 and they are still friends today. Gary worked at the factory for almost three years in the Power Slot of the assembly process, testing props, engine combinations, LP fueled diesel engines and 305 to 460 cubic inch displaced motors. He always looked for ways to improve the engines and boat performance.

Rob's first assignment for Gary was to perform a time study on each stage of the production line. Gary remembered how that task went over with the good old boys from Blount County, Tennessee when they saw a kid show up with a stopwatch and a clipboard to watch everything they did. They didn't know whether to work fast or slow up. Gary took his notes and times up to Rob. Rob saw that if we gave the first station on the line another drill it would save two minutes because he did not have to change drill bits.

Mr. Fowler, who went by the nickname "Fud," was the most senior employee on that station. Fud saw that the extra drill was going to make it easier for him. Fud passed the word up the assembly line that Gary was "good to go" with the rest of the line. The new kid became the new team member and was immediately accepted into the closed association of men who worked with pride and a sense of purpose. Rob knew that would happen.

Gary realized that the real advantage MasterCraft had at that time was the ability to make quick changes and adopt innovative ideas by executive decision. The corporate competition had many more levels of approval to go through before a change could be implemented. Rob Shirley was a committee of one whose approval was faster. MasterCraft workers were always testing, trying something new while producing 20 boats a week, two shifts a day in the fiberglass shop. There were seven hull molds utilizing one shift a day in the rigging shop where they built four boats a day every five days. Today, MasterCraft builds fifteen boats a day and has forty-three qualities controlled checkpoints where the space-age technology of the modern boats is rigorously and meticulously inspected. The smallest glitch can halt today's assembly line until the "glitch" is identified, fixed or dealt with by a supervising technician. Only then will the assembly line begin to move.

Gary's assignment included testing every boat that came off the line on the lake Rob built next to the factory. That lake had special significance to Rob. He built the lake in order to test boats and avoid constantly traveling 10 mile away each time a boat was tested. He dug the lake and a flowing spring opened up in the adjacent farmer's field and flooded his corn crop. Rob placed Gary in charge of draining the lake and lining the bottom with a layer of clay in order to stop the leak.

Gary's responsibility was to create the first test sheet checklist. Most of the boats needed nothing because the production quality was excellent. But, every once and a while when the plant would get a new employee assigned to installing driveshaft logs, every one of them would leak until the man developed installation skills. During the learning curve, every boat would go back to the line for repairs.

GARY MAHLER

Gary was close to Rob's family. He worked down stairs in the plant, while Rob and his family used to live upstairs. Gary watched Rob's children, Mike and Jill come down the spiral staircase to go to school every day. Rob's Great Danes were outside.

Gary recalls that those were the early days during the cutting edge of ski boat innovation and competitive water skiing was growing at a rapid pace. Several programs began in the seventies. The MasterCraft reunion at Cypress Gardens, the Coors Light Pro Ski tour, The MercCruiser Jump Classic with a Inboard/Outboard powered boat that pulled a new world Jump Record of 187-feet beating Wayne Grimditch's old record by seven feet.

Gary was still a kid just out of college. He was excited to be a part of a team that broke a world record. To Gary, it was a big deal. Gary recalls the MercCruiser tech representative in charge of fitting, servicing and changing propellers showing up in Tyler, Texas with a trailer filled with 300 propellers. Rob inspected his supply to see if he had anything better. He found on prop that Rob used a hammer and a trailer hitch ball to "hammer more cup" in the propeller to control slippage. Jack Walker drove that boat that day, and called it "The Tyler Wiggle" for the loose linkages that always haunted stern drive performances.

And then, Rob started building MasterCraft Skis. Rob got tired of putting up all the money for pro tournaments and the only picture you would see was the winner holding up a ski with no mention of the boat company that had actually made the tournament happen.

Kris and Bob LaPoint were on the MasterCraft pro team, so they were asked to come up with a high-end slalom ski prototype. Kris was always working on a better ski design anyway. Ski design is a job that is never finished. Like ski boats, there is always room for improvement.

Bob LaPoint showed up at the Team Trials for Masters Tournament at Calloway Gardens that year with MasterCraft slalom. He kept the fin covered until it was under water and everyone wanted to know what he had on that new slalom. It was the first of the winged fins that Bob tested at Diesel John's Butterfly Lake under secrecy, weeks before.

The crew at the factory assembled skis and polished those gold winged fins right next to the boat production line, and Rob sold them to the dealers across the world. Rob would ship containers of boats overseas with skis, vests and shirts packed inside the boats.

The early overseas shipments went on deck of the big ships, because of the cost savings. Unfortunately, the boats would arrive at their destination stripped of all removable parts and just become an insurance claim at the receiving end of the trip.

Gary took one boat with a special trailer that had to have a folding tongue that was bound for King Hussein in Jordon, and dropped it off at JFK air cargo in New York where it was loaded in the front of a 747. The folding trailer tongue made the turn possible for the cargo door to close.

Rob trusted Gary with a free reign to go to any ski tournament or show that he felt would give MasterCraft the best exposure. Gary was on the road 40 weekends a year. Such travel took its toll. Gary remembers calling Rob from the first barefoot Nationals in Ocala, Florida where MasterCraft had made a special PCM powered 454 with a custom prop, just for that boat and that tournament. It was a 53 mph speedster. Somebody on site took it for an unauthorized joyride after Gary left and bent a push rod. Gary had to return to the tournament site to make the repairs. Luckily, Gary found the parts locally.

But, that was it for Gary. He called Rob and said, "I have had only three days off in the past five months, and I'm going to take some time off." Rob simply said, "Go ahead, see you when you get back." Rob had long ago put Gary on salary because he drove to so many tournaments and worked so many overtime hours.

On the few weekends Gary was in Maryville, he and Rob would go dirt biking into the Smokey Mountains around the plant. One year they went to Daytona for bike week and rode in the Alligator Enduro event with Bob LaPoint, Greg Davis, and Fred Hardwick. They hauled the bikes behind the custom MasterCraft GMC coach with a custom molded fiberglass six- bike MasterCraft motorcycle trailer and had a fun-filled weekend.

Gary recalls taking a ride in the van with Rob in 1981 and told him, "Rob, I love the job, the people, and the sport. But, I need to live somewhere other than Maryville."

Rob's comment was, "I wondered how long you would last." Gary moved back to South Florida on Lake Eden, remained on the promo team until 1998, when Rob started Infinity Ski Boats.

That is a story for another book.

Gary graduated from New England College in 1977 and went to work for MasterCraft Boat Company where he worked for three years as National Promotional Team Coordinator, National Sales Manager of MasterCraft Skis and in Research and Development. He was involved in the innovation of the "Power Slot" and wrote an article about this hull change and its benefits for the 1980 Volume 4, Issue 4 of Spray Magazine that featured a cover shot of Joel McClintock.

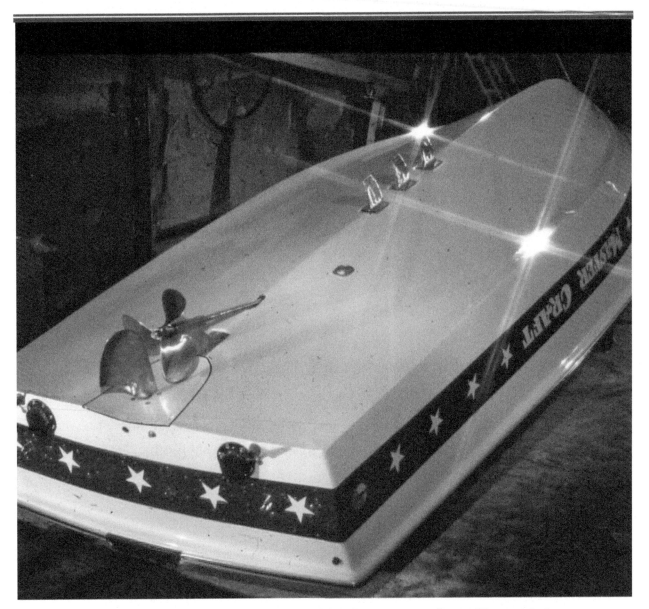

THE POWER SLOT MASTERCRAFT HULL DESIGN WAS GARY MAHLER'S IDEA

He left Tennessee after three years and founded Master Mark Hot Air Systems that were the original boat heaters used in competition ski boats. He also was involved in the Satellite TV Business at that time. He later sold the heater business to George Taylor.

At one time, Gary was a member of the Greater Miami Ski Club, Ski Club of the Palm Beaches and the Gold Coast Ski Club. He became a Senior Judge and Senior Driver, Designated Driver Examiner and he remains an Emeritus Driver. Gary was a Chief Driver of two Southern Regionals, drove the Junior Worlds in Greece, the Americas challenge in Edmonton and also Winnipeg and the Pam American's in Santiago, Chile.

He served many years as councilman for the state of Florida, and is an Honorary National Director after serving for six years as a Director of the Southern Region. He also served four years as an alternate for AWSA to the USOC and was Vice President of AWSA for two years. Gary was President of the Ski Club of the Palm Beaches in 1989, which was the year the World Championships were held in West Palm.

Gary started Infinity Ski Boats in 1989 with Rob Shirley, Kris LaPoint and Mike Shirley and built the first boat to ever qualify for the National Championships in its first year of production. The company closed in 2002.

Gary's water ski accomplishments include running 2 at 38 feet off in the Bakersfield Nationals and Gary was a part of the team that has the record for skiing the most courses in one day behind the same boat! (17 or 18 courses?) Over the years Gary skied in numerous National tournaments.

Gary retired from water skiing in 2005 but supports AWSEF and goes to Hall of Fame functions whenever old friends or acquaintances are honored. He has donated several items to the HOF, including a mirror etched with a MasterCraft that includes pictures of the team skiers.

CHAPTER NINETEEN

BIG CHANGES WITH COLLATERAL DAMAGE

By 1984, Rob Shirley was physically and mentally exhausted. The international travel with the pro tour combined with the boat building industry had completely taken over Rob's life. After taking the entire year to make his decision, Rob sold his interest in the pro tour and MasterCraft Boats. He felt it was time to step aside and let a more powerful entity; The Coleman Group (Camping equipment) take over and push MasterCraft to the next level.

MR. AND MRS. SHELDON COLEMAN WITH ROB SHIRLEY

Sheldon Coleman was a really good man. During the year that Rob contemplated selling MasterCraft, Sheldon came to the plant many times to visit. He had the remarkable ability to remember people's names and would spend time on the assembly room floor. Rob remembered a day when Mr. Coleman said to a worker, "Hey, Joe, how are your wife and kids? You'll still be here on my next visit, won't you?"

Mr. Coleman told Rob, "I don't know how to make anything, but I really like people." Rob made the decision to sell MasterCraft, and within minutes after the deal closed, Rob was overcome with the heavy regret of Seller's Remorse. Rob thought, "What have I done to my company?"

During the weeks and months after the sale, MasterCraft began slipping in sales. Production slowed and workers soon had their time cut or suffered layoffs. MasterCraft was losing market share to other brands and to manufacturers in the ski boat and growing wakeboard industry. Not long after the sale, Mr. Coleman sold the majority of his stock in the company and it led to him being forced out of his own companies.

Unfortunately, it also ended the special bond Rob had with MasterCraft, the company he had founded with his bare hands. Rob also lost touch with many others who had helped him along the way. MasterCraft boats found itself buried in the morass of bureaucracy that was the Wall Street game. Rob got as far away from the business as possible.

Rob moved to the Cayman Islands and took up the sport of scuba diving in 1985. He also never lost his love for riding dirt bikes. He entered a race in South America called The Trans Amazon Rally in 1988. It was a race from Colombia to Argentina that it took a year to train, prepare for and plan.

Rob hired Dick Burlson to set up two bikes for the event. Dick is a former World Champion Enduro Rider. He did an amazing job for Rob and provided Rob with an even more amazing experience that took 26 days and cost him a few broken ribs, fingers and his nose. It required a month to heal afterwards.

Rob rode through the Amazon Region and crossed the border of Colombia into Ecuador, Peru, Chile and on into Argentina. He endured the jungles, swamps and critters of the Amazon as well as the thin air atop the Andes Mountain Range of southern South America. It was all worth it to a competitor like Rob Shirley. He won the motorcycle division in the 9000-mile race.

The next year Rob entered a race in Australia. He tore a cruciate ligament in his knee that added serious downtime to his other adventures. But, the following year, Rob climbed back on his bike and entered a race in the Dominican Republic. He finished that race trailing well behind the eventual winner and decided that it was time to end his racing career.

And now, Rob rides for fun sticking to off-road rides only. "Streets are too dangerous, and not very much fun," Rob laments. He says, "I enjoy dual sport riding, camping and photography, always looking for wild animals to shoot...with my camera, of course."

CHAPTER TWENTY

"LIVING THE DREAM."

Rob returned to the Cayman Islands and began the development of a real estate project called BONNIE'S ARCH, a condominium development in 1989. That turned out pretty well, so Rob entered into another venture.

His interest in the condo project dominated most of his time and it was only natural that a boat builder with a background like Rob had would become interested in building a better boat. Rob decided he would build a special dive boat that commercial dive shops could use to take divers out on scuba and snorkeling excursions. Like The MasterCraft, Rob felt he had a unique design for a specialty dive boat. He jumped into the new dive boat construction with both feet running, as is Rob's style.

Rob spent the greater part of 1990 designing a custom 42-foot dive boat under the trade name ROB SHIRLEY CUSTOM BOATS. Rob was confident that with his experience in marketing it would be natural to conclude that he would be successful promoting his new boat design to dive shops around the world. At that time there were no commercial dive boats especially rigged for the needs of dive shops that were available to buy.

Rob set up a shop in Key West, Florida and began the construction of 42-foot and 48-foot custom dive boats. Rob built 125 special boats for customers located from the South Pacific to the Middle East. Life for Rob became interesting again as he sold and delivered boats all over the world, and went diving in some of the most beautiful waters on the planet.

Mike Shirley

MIKE SHIRLEY IS NOW A DESIGN ENGINEER WITH SUPRA BOATS

It was during this period of time that Rob's son Mike graduated from Florida State University with exceptional qualifications in computers and engineering. A company based in Ohio hired Mike Shirley right out of college. Mike had grown up in the shadow of the Master-Craft factory and had developed a great work ethic that he combined with his exceptional educational discipline. Rob invited Mike to come to Key West to come and take a look at what his Dad was doing.

Early in his life, Mike inherited his Dad's passion for diving and already had the love for boating buried deep in his DNA. Mike decided to leave the Ohio Company and join his father in the dive boat manufacturing business in Key West. During Mike's formative years, Rob spent an inordinate amount of time away from his family in pursuit of his massive MasterCraft successes. This new opportunity would be a great chance to pursue a Father and Son Project. It worked out so well that Mike took over the engineering and actual building of the boats and freed Rob up to spend more time promoting, marketing, selling and delivering boats. Rob sent boats to far off destinations on the decks and in the holds of ships. Rob would travel to each destination where the new dive boats were delivered. He would assemble the boat and train the buyers on how to take care of their new, one-of-a-kind dive boats. In most cases, the boats were in remote areas of the world. Only five boats were sold inside the continental United States.

Back in Maryville, Tennessee, MasterCraft Boat Company had a problem. The newest president of the company called Mike and asked if he and Rob could travel to Tennessee to help fix the problem. MasterCraft boats failed to pass the performance test for USA Water Ski, and would not be used in sanctioned tournaments for that year. As Mike told Rob the news, Rob replied, "My God! We set the standards. That was unheard of."

Rob flew to Knoxville and drove to Maryville and visited his old MasterCraft Factory. The problem didn't take long for an expert like Rob to identify. His research showed that the changes that the company had made to the running surfaces of the MasterCraft boats caused severe handling problems. Rob called on pro slalom skier, Kris LaPoint to assist in trying to save that year's fleet of boats that had already been molded, built and a lot of them had been shipped to dealers already.

Rob informed the MasterCraft executives that the hull molds would have to be replaced and it was anyone's guess what to do with the boats that had already been built.

MasterCraft was not satisfied with Rob's assessment of the problem and told Rob to try harder by coming up with some add-on device that might make the problem appear to go away.

Rob and Kris experimented with a rudder design that helped with steering, but it placed an additional drag on the hull causing a drop in the top-end speed of the boat and increased the amount of fuel consumption. MasterCraft executives made the decision to use the new rudder on the existing inventory of boats and asked Rob and Kris to come up with a new hull design for the following season.

Starting from scratch, Rob and Kris took their "out of the box" approach to a new design. MasterCraft rejected their design. As the CEO told Rob, "It is too far from standard designs, and too much of a change." The project was scrapped.

Rob considered it a big letdown. He returned to his own dive boat business and tried to forget MasterCraft. "We did our best for them," Rob said. Almost a year later, Rob was contacted by several of his former dealer friends who suggested that he consider getting back in the ski boat building business since Rob already had a boat manufacturing factory going again.

Rob was reluctant to get back into the business of ski boat manufacturing at first. But then, Rob used his experience to perform what is called a Survey of Due Diligence and found that all the market indicators were in place for a new success. Rob received orders from dealers for 250 of whatever boat he decided to design and build. He determined that it would cost over four million dollars to do the project and his competition would now be MasterCraft, Correct Craft and Malibu boats.

CHAPTER TWENTY ONE

FROM THE ASHES OF DESPAIR

Rob Shirley, Mike Shirley, Kris LaPoint and Gary Mahler spent the next 6 months designing, building and launching a new ski boat called The Infinity. They registered the name, built the first prototype and were very excited about the result of their work and the look, feel and performance of the new boat.

"I returned to the ski boat industry because many of you wanted me to come up with some new innovations which would help boost the sport to a higher level. The Infinity ZX-I does everything right. Test one for yourself."
— Rob Shirley

Rob started the new plant from scratch. They trained new employees, built molds and started production. From a zero inventory they built 500 Infinity special competition ski boats. The market was ready for a new and better boat. Ski tournament officials welcomed the new boat and performances of skiers indicated that they loved skiing behind the new boat.

A 2002 ADVERTISEMENT FOR THE INFINITY

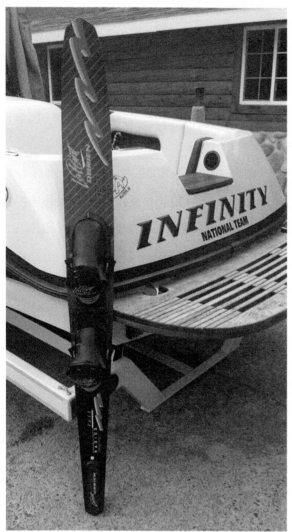

INFINITY DREAM THAT ENDED ON 9/11/01
KRIS LaPOINT'S PERSONAL INFINITY

Rob was reading the reviews of the boat and sat in his living room on Tuesday morning, September 11, 2001. It was just after 8:00am when Rob glanced up at the TV to see the commotion on the TODAY SHOW and saw the pictures of the World Trade Center in New York City burning from an apparent plane crash. He watched the screen and tried to make sense out of how something like that could happen, when the second airliner crashed into the adjacent building of the World Trade Center.

Rob's instinctive mind told him that his, and everyone else's world had changed in that devastating moment. He watched as the cameras scanned the buildings from afar until the network producers realized that all of their viewing audience could see the people who were jumping out of the destruction and falling to their death on the sidewalks and streets below.

Rob, along with all Americans, was in shock, and dropped his eyes from the screen in sorrow.

The reaction to the atrocity in New York was immediate for many people in the business of travel, entertainment and boating, especially in the water ski business. What was once a growing water sport became instantly unimportant in the face of what was becoming a threat to the safety and security of the American Public, and to the rest of the world.

The collateral damage from the September 11, 2001 terrorist attack forced the closing of many famous dive shops in all parts of the world. Travel was severely restricted. Tourism dried up. Ski boat dealers canceled all of their orders for ski boats and the Infinity project was forced to go "belly up." The inventory was surely going to be repossessed. The Infinity investors were going to lose 4 million dollars and Rob was forced into a position of economic incarceration overnight. Not only did Rob lose the fortune he had gained from the sale of MasterCraft Boats, he lost his investment, equity and future in his two new boat companies, along with the good faith, money and credit of his Infinity and Dive Boat investors as the orders for his new boats were cancelled by the dealers, one after the other.

Rob sunk into a deep depression. He was 62 years old. Because of the terrorist acts of despots from around the globe, Rob felt sorrow for those who lost lives, and he felt the most oppressive sorrow for those who trusted his judgment. Rob felt he had let them down. The weight of depression is deeper and darker than an unmarked grave and carries a lasting burden that, to an entrepreneur like Rob, feels a whole lot like shame.

It was not deserved. Rob did everything right.

CHAPTER TWENTY TWO

SURVIVAL OF THE SPIRIT

Rob visited Colombia, Belize. Costa Rica, Honduras and Panama looking for economical places to live. His only remaining funds were from the proceeds from the sale of his personal residence. Panama in the Central American Republic became the best choice due to its growing economy. He bought a modest home in the rain forest where there are good dirt bike trails and where he lives with his wife, Nubia and his black Labrador, Bobo.

It is entirely conjecture and speculation by the medical professionals that attended to Rob after Nubia found him unconscious in their Panama home in January, 2015. He was rushed to a Panama City hospital in a comatose state where he remained in the Intensive Care Unit for 15 days. Rob's son Mike and daughter Jill flew to Panama to help. Due to equipment that did not work or was not available, a Medivac jet from Grand Cayman transported Rob with two doctors on board, to the Medical Center at the University of Tennessee. Rob remained in the ICU for another week.

GENEROUS, LOYAL AND TRUSTED FRIENDS BROUGHT ROB BACK TO KNOXVILLE AND SAVED HIS LIFE

He awoke from his coma in serious condition after being totally unresponsive for so long. Speech was impossible, and movement of atrophied muscles nearly as bad. After Rob was removed from life support, he was transferred to a rehabilitation facility to begin the slow process of recovery. The doctors have never come up with any diagnosis for the coma. Tropical insect bites to exotic venoms were ruled out as a cause but nothing was ever determined or ruled in as a cause.

Thanks to his family, and the nurses at the rehab center who performed miracles by retraining Rob's body to finally rise from his bed and walk to the bathroom again, and the loyal and faithful friends who made the trip to Tennessee possible.

Those friends saved a good man's life.

EPILOGUE

ROB FORGES A STREAM IN NEAR HIS HOME IN TROPICAL CENTRAL AMERICAN PANAMA

Rob is back in the rain forest with Nubia, Bobo and his dirt bike again.

His pace is slower, and his view of the wildlife in the forest last a lot longer. He has even managed to see two black panthers while riding his dirt bike. He wears boots to ward off deadly snakebites, a jump suit and helmet to protect him from insects, but not the heat. His camera is always at the ready for a colorful bird.

Rob hasn't owned a boat in over ten years. He has recovered his health and is regaining his strength. At nearly 75 years old, Rob says, "I still miss the old days. But, I am closer to my grown children than I have ever been. My son, Mike, (Now a design engineer at Supra boats) and my daughter, Jill (Cable) gave me two grandchildren that I enjoy immensely, Rachel Cable (18) and Adam Shirley (13).

Rob's parting statement to his doctors as he left the Medical Center to return to Panama was,

"What a life! I wouldn't change a thing."

NEVER QUIT

(ROB WOULDN'T ALLOW THE AUTHOR TO SAY "THE END")

PREVIEWS OF COMING ATTRACTIONS

The Future of towed wake sports rests in the hands of a new generation of athletes like Harley Clifford. Take a look over the horizon into the future of MasterCraft Boats as athletes in all nine disciplines seek new levels of excellence. Harley Clifford hits a perfect wakeboard pass and is awarded a perfect score for his excellent effort.

PHOTO COURTESY OF LYNN NOVAKOFSKI, USA WATER SKI MAGAZINE.

Whatever your chosen water sport discipline is, MasterCraft Boats has a boat that will perfectly fit your style. For the three-event water skier, wake-boarders, barefoot skiers, show skiers, wake-skaters, wake-surfers and skiers with disabilities; MasterCraft has a boat for you.

THE 2016 MASTERCRAFT LINE OF BOATS

MASTERCRAFT PROSTAR

MASTERCRAFT X26

MASTERCRAFT X20

MASTERCRAFT X10

MASTERCRAFT X23

Worldwide boat manufacturers are building approximately 12,000 water ski specialty inboard boats a year. MasterCraft can expect their fair share of the world's ski boat annual sales. But the boat of the future is the wake and surf specialty boats that now number well over 10 times the number of water ski boats produced. MasterCraft will sell more wake and surf specialty boats as the future of towed water sports continues to attract enthusiasts from all over the world. They are preparing the molds now for a state-of-the-art 26 footer with space-aged technology and top-of-the-line fittings and equipment.

Enjoy your retirement Rob. The MasterCraft Boat Company is in good hands and will remain a major supplier of superior quality boats for all of the towed water sports enthusiasts regardless of whether they are recreational riders or world champions in any of the popular disciplines.

MASTERCRAFT THROUGH THE YEARS

1968 MASTERCRAFT-The original

1973 MASTERCRAFT

One of 54 boats produced, belongs to Paul Hickman

Cleveland, Tennessee

1975 MASTERCRAFT

1976

ALAN AND ROBBIE KEMPTON'S BI-CENTENNIAL SPECIAL EDITION MASTERCRAFT

1977 MASTERCRAFT

OWNED BY PETER AND LUKE BIEVER

ST. PAUL, MN

1978 MASTERCRAFT

1979 MASTERCRAFT

1986 MASTERCRAFT

1986 MASTERCRAFT

1988 MASTERCRAFT

1988 MASTERCRAFT OUTBOARD

1991 MASTERCRAFT OUTBOARD

1993 MASTERCRAFT

ONE OF SEVERAL BOATS BELONGING TO CHUCK BRUMLEY

KINGSTON, TENNESSEE

1995 MASTERCRAFT

1996 MASTERCRAFT

USAF PILOT MAJOR WESTON HOEPER & KRISTA HOEPER'S 2002 PROSTAR 197 ARE TYPICAL MASTERCRAFT CUSTOMERS, ENJOYING A DAY WITH THEIR CHILDREN, HOLLY, ETHAN AND BOYD ON LAKE DELTON, AT WISCONSIN DELLS, WS

THANKS TO ROB SHIRLEY AND MASTERCRAFT BOATS FOR ALL YOU HAVE DONE FOR OUR FAMILY.

A VERY SPECIAL THANKS TO WESTON HOEPER FOR ALL HE HAS DONE FOR ALL OF OUR FRIENDS, FAMILIES AND CUSTOMERS WORLDWIDE. THANK YOU FOR YOUR SERVICE MAJOR.

ROB SHIRLEY, FOUNDER
TERRY MCNEW, CEO
MASTERCRAFT BOAT COMPANY

About the Author

Jon Broderick, was born in Toledo, Ohio and grew up water skiing on Clark Lake, Michigan in the summers. He went on to make the team at Cypress Gardens, Florida to become a performer in the water ski shows made famous there, and go on to build his own attractions and ski shows in Cape Coral, Florida, Townsend, Tennessee and San Antonio, Texas before finally retiring, earning a Master's Degree in Creative Writing and becoming an author at the age of 74.

BOOKS BY JON BRODERICK

WATER SKIING LEGEND
THE LIFE AND TIMES OF
FRANK BONNEY

PTSD NO APOLOGIES –ANTHOLOGY

DYING DREAMS

A DIAMOND IN THE ROUGH

FIVE MILES DEEP

TIGER SHARK TERROR

TOTEM

CPSIA information can be obtained
at www.ICGtesting.com
Printed in the USA
LVOW05s0728220316

480217LV00018B/80/P

9 781936 617326